STOLEN
LIVES

STOLEN LIVES

Identity Theft
Prevention Made Simple

John D. Sileo

DaVinci Publishing • Denver, Colorado

To order copies or to request permission to reprint, contact the publisher at
DaVinci Publishing, 381 S. Broadway, Denver, CO 80209
or email: orders@thinklikeaspy.com

ISBN 0-9770597-7-4

Library of Congress Control Number: 2005906543

Publisher's Cataloging-in-Publication Data

Sileo, John D.
    Stolen lives : identity theft prevention made simple / John D. Sileo.
    p. cm.
    Includes bibliographical references and index.
    ISBN 0-9770597-7-4

1. Identity theft—United States. 2. Identity theft—United States—Prevention. 3. Credit card fraud—United States. 4. Fraud—United States. 5. Consumer protection—United States. 6. Privacy, right of—United States. I. Title.
HV6679 .S55
2005906543
364.163—dc22

Printed in the United States of America.

DaVinci Publishing
381 S. Broadway
Denver, CO 80209

Read first...

Stolen Life #1: The Author's Story

At first, I stole only small amounts, mostly from people I knew.

I'd pay for a cup of coffee or take a friend to lunch and pay with other people's money. But my newfound prosperity drew me in, and I grew bolder. Imagine owning your dreams—vacations, cars, gifts, fancy restaurants—without having to work for them. It was like winning the lotto every day.

My methods were simple. I charged everything on a credit card. To pay off the card, I would steal account numbers off of the bottom of people's checks and electronically transfer the funds into my account. Everyone seemed too busy and distracted to notice money disappearing from their lives.

I took small precautions, but most of my victims were too overwhelmed with life to notice cash being siphoned out of their bank. I thought, "If they are this lazy about their checking accounts, I'll never get caught."

By my sixteenth month and $295,000 later, I was hooked. But I'd gotten greedy and reckless and was now transferring more than $20,000 a month from many sources. And the wrong person finally woke up.

By the time this book is published, I will have been sentenced, jailed and released. Thanks to plea bargaining, I will be given a 30-day jail sentence, which will be commuted to 18 days—just enough time to plan my next scheme.

But don't worry, I have learned from my mistakes. Now I know how to fully take advantage of people who insist on burying their heads in the sand when it comes to identity theft. Next time, I won't get caught...

This story is true. The crimes are real. But I didn't commit them—an identity thief did.

I am the victim. Yet, ironically, I now know what it feels like to be a thief. On many occasions, when your identity is stolen, you become the thief! If you were confused over whose voice is telling the above story, consider how confusing your life will become when someone has your identity! It is the victim who is often investigated and treated like a thief. At times, you even begin to feel like a thief.

You see, when your identity is stolen and used to commit fraud, everyone (the police, your bank, your creditors, the government and occasionally friends and family) assumes that:

- you committed the crime
- you filed for bankruptcy
- you paid for the drugs
- you hijacked the plane
- you defaulted on the loan
- you owe the money

…until you prove otherwise. And because there is no federal agency tasked with sorting out whether you're the victim or the thief, you are mostly alone on that journey.

It was 16 months after my identity had been stolen that a government investigator knocked on my door and recommended that I find a criminal lawyer. That was the first time I knew my identity had been stolen.

And, for the next two years, I felt I was living a stolen life.

Had I taken the simplest of precautions, even just those discussed in *Plan B* of this book (page 115), I would have prevented:

- **500 hours** spent recovering $300,000 in losses
- **$9,000** in attorney's fees to keep myself out of jail
- The **humiliation** of friends and family wondering if I was a criminal
- The **hassle** of rebuilding my credit history, one creditor at a time

- The **paperwork**, oh, the paperwork (police reports, affidavits, letters…)
- Hundreds of **lost hours of productivity at work** while I recovered my identity during working hours (banks and credit bureaus close at 5 p.m.)
- The **bitterness** that grows from being viewed as guilty until I was able to prove myself innocent

What I fear is being in the presence of evil and doing nothing. I fear that more than death.

— Otilia De Koster, *Newsweek* (12/19/1988)

Exhausted from the battle, and certain that lightning doesn't strike twice, I took almost no steps to protect myself, and my identity was stolen a second time by someone rooting through my garbage. This time I was "luckier." My "other" identity simply moved to another state, opened a bank account, took out a loan and wrote some bad checks. She (yes, that's correct, a woman stole my identity) disappeared before she was able to complete a bankruptcy on my Social Security number. This episode of identity theft destroyed my newly recovered credit, but that only took six months to sort out.

The precautions I have taken to keep lightning from striking a third time are the subject of this book. It is my attempt to keep as many people as possible from experiencing the stress and pain that has overwhelmed my family and me for the past two years. And, while most victims of identity theft won't go through the same nightmarish experience I did, there always is pain.

During those years in the trenches of recovery, I learned a great deal about prevention firsthand—from attorneys, judges, sheriffs, detectives, district attorneys, the FBI, the Secret Service, and Postal Inspectors—as well as through extensive research.

My goal is to use this knowledge to keep others from experiencing stolen lives and to make prevention a lasting habit.

Dedicated to:

Mary—
my anchor and compass,
comedian and muse.
You have my heart.

Sophia and Makayla—
the only purpose I will ever need in life.

Mom, Dad and Andrea—
the reason I've never once felt alone.

Acknowledgements

I did not write this book alone. I share the honor with many others:

To my wife Mary, who deserves more credit than I do for this book. While I was off writing, she was caring beautifully for our family, teaching classes and editing *Stolen Lives*. Thank you, My Love.

To my early readers and coaches—Barbara Sileo, Jim Sileo, C.R. Sturgis, Peter Jacobson, Ken McGuigan and Ben Kuruvila.

To my outstanding editor, Barbara Munson.

To my publicist and close friend, Andrea Throndson.

To Michael Zinanti, my extra self-esteem as an author, father, husband and friend.

To my invaluable sounding boards—Kathleen Keelan, Pat Lencioni, Michael Zinanti, Eric Peacock, Karen Peacock, Seth Jacobson, Sara Zimmerman, Richard Broach, Steven Bellio, Elisabeth Jacobson, Madeline McIntosh, Dan Poynter, Mark Sanborn, Jordan Goodman, Greg Godek, Alethea Black, Ric Giardina, John Carroll, Michael Santarlangelo, II, Jennifer M. de St. Georges, Barbara McNichol, Dee Dukeheart, Janet Steward, Bob Cox, Jack Jobe, Margaret Maupin, Cathy Langer, Kristin Mavis, Joe Sabah, Christine & Pat Connolly, Todd Vanosdoll, Lesley Batchelor, Nikki Denton, Ron King, Dr. Bill Crowley, Billy Crowley, Chris Rogers, Christian Meyer, Andrea Throndson, Geoff Watson, Mike Pramenko, and everyone else who took time out of their busy lives to help me. Thank you for your patience and friendship.

A special thank you to Jim Van Dyke, Don Phan, Colette Woodruff, and everyone at Javelin Strategy & Research for your wonderful reports, sound methodology and ongoing help. Your accuracy and care make this a better book.

Identity fraud cost the United States $52.6 billion last year.

An estimated 9.3 million people became victims.

For the "average" person, preventing identity theft is the same as saving $5,686.[1]

Contents

A [9/11] hijacker identified as Abdulaziz Alomari... was reported by the Rocky Mountain News *to have the same name as a graduate of the University of Colorado... Investigators subsequently learned that in 1995 the Colorado student had reported a theft in his apartment; among the items stolen was his passport... Social Security officials also said that six of the nineteen hijackers were using identity cards belonging to other people.*

—*Seymour Hersh,* The New Yorker, *6/3/2002*

How to Protect:

How to:

Other:

Introduction

Am I at Risk?
A Two-Minute Litmus Test

The scenarios below will test your readiness to prevent identity theft. There is not necessarily one right answer to these situations; use them as a barometer of how prepared you are to handle similar situations. If you are uncertain about any of the answers, then you will benefit significantly from this book.

☐ Someone asks you to name 40 or more pieces of private information that make up your identity. Can you name them?

☐ Someone asks you to name the most common forms of identity theft and who generally commits the crimes (according to statistics, not media coverage).

☐ Someone close to you has his or her identity stolen and it makes you want to take action for yourself. Are you better off scheduling one entire weekend to protect yourself or doing it slowly, taking it one step at a time?

☐ You received an email from a friend telling you to not sign your credit card. Instead, he tells you to write "See Photo ID" on the signature line. Do you follow his instructions or does this nullify your credit card agreement?

☐ You receive convenience checks from your credit card company in the mail. What do you do with them?

☐ You are donating office computers to a local charity. They have been sitting in a back room for months. What do you do before they are picked up?

☐ You are ordering new checks through the mail. Where should the checks be delivered?

☐ You receive an email from your bank suggesting that your account may have been fraudulently accessed. They need you to verify your

15

information on their website to protect you. They ask you to click on the link to the bank's website. How do you respond?

☐ You are paying your monthly bills. Do you put the checks in your home mailbox or in the blue USPS box in front of the post office? Do you have other choices?

☐ Your computer provider says that you need a firewall, anti-virus protection, anti-spyware protection or Windows updates to make your computer safe. It will cost several hundred dollars. Do you take their advice?

☐ Your bank contacts you and practically begs you to move to online statements. You feel that they just want to save postage and printing costs. Do you follow their advice?

☐ You are having dinner at a local restaurant. It is time to pay the bill and you will be using a credit card. The card will be taken into the back room by the waiter to be run through the credit card machine. Do you let it disappear?

☐ You are buying clothes at a department store. They offer to save you 10% on this purchase if you sign up for their credit card. Do you take the offer?

☐ You are buying a new car and financing the loan. The car dealer needs your Social Security number to process the loan. Do you give it to him or her?

☐ A technician from the company that repairs your computers at work calls asking for simple, public information. Do you give it to him or her?

☐ You've lost your wallet and can't remember what it contained. What steps do you take?

Where to Start?

There are several ways to read this book. Choose the method that best fits with your lifestyle and how you get work done.

1. **The Scholar.** The book includes Mindsets and Action Items. Read it cover to cover, learning the Mindsets and completing each set of Action Items as you read. Because each Mindset is practiced several times using the Action Items, you will tend to come away with a better grasp of thinking like a spy—the person who is intent on stealing your identity! You also will have all the tools to protect your identity.

2. **The Pragmatist.** Read it from start to finish, but only read (and don't complete) the tasks (Action Items) as you go. When you have finished, turn to Chapter 12, *Your Calendar of Prevention,* in the back of this book. Here, the tasks are prioritized so you are performing the most important ones first. This style works if you are dedicated to doing the heavy work (the Action Items) after you have already completed the knowledge work (the Mindsets). By using the calendar, you are setting yourself on a scheduled course to safety.

3. **The Doer.** If you are eager to get going and don't have time to read through the book now, jump directly to *Your Calendar of Prevention.* There, you will find a prioritized list of small, manageable steps to take. Then, as you have time, return to each chapter to learn the Mindsets. This is the quickest way to start short-term prevention, though it may be a more difficult way to develop lasting habits.

Please understand that there is a lot of valuable information in this book. It will take time to complete the action items and make habits of the mindsets. If you are tempted to only do the Calendar of Prevention, you will be helping yourself immensely now, but without establishing an identity theft prevention mindset that becomes a habit over time, you will find yourself slipping, forgetting and eventually again running the risk of becoming victimized.

Regardless of your method, **GET STARTED**.

Getting started is more important than finishing everything. Learning to think about and guard your privacy is more important than completing the calendar quickly. In the meantime, follow your instincts.

Finally, please use this book as a workbook. Where I have left out information that is pertinent to your situation, add it. Highlight the tasks that you need to act on and check items off as you complete them.

Preventing identity theft is an interactive process that requires you to *do* something, not just read a book. Use this book as your first tool for taking action.

Identity theft can happen to anyone! It has little to do with how much or how little money you have. The average identity theft victim has an average income and leads an average life.

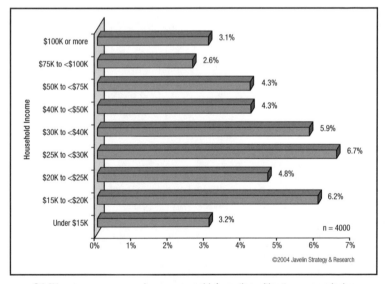

QA "Has anyone ever used your personal information without your permission to obtain new credit cards, new bank accounts or loans in your name, run up debts in your name, open other new accounts, or otherwise commit theft, fraud, or some other crime?"

1

Your Identity Is Your Most Valuable Asset

When I am speaking to audiences about identity theft, they tend to react like I used to: *"I will listen, but I don't need to act, because it won't happen to me."* They are alarmingly disconnected from the immediate reality of identity theft. I tell them that if they don't take significant steps to protect themselves, they have roughly a **1 in 10 chance of having their identity stolen** in the next two years. A few of them begin to listen.

Then I ask another question: "If someone were to tell you that your home has a 1 in 10 chance of being robbed every other year, would you take steps to prevent it from happening?"

"ABSOLUTELY!" they answer.

Sometimes I have to point out the irony that the valuables in their home, and even their home itself, are *always* worth less than their identity, which is made up of all of their assets combined.

Many people spend $800 a year on a security system protecting their $300,000 house. They spend $1,100 on home insurance without blinking. They have car alarms installed for $500, carry auto insurance in case their car is stolen and even spend $5 on a combination lock for the gym.

But most people spend very little money and time protecting their **most valuable financial asset, their identity**. Ironically, securing your identity can be done with little time and money. The cost of this book and of implementing the necessary changes is immaterial compared to the costs of recovering from identity theft.

Why are we so complacent about the safety of our identity? Because we have been lulled into giving away our private information, one "insignificant" piece at a time. Like a frog in the cooking pot, we don't notice we are being boiled alive because the changes in temperature are so incremental.

And no one has taught us how to stop giving away our identities. The books I've read and lectures I've attended while researching this book were mostly laundry lists of steps we must take to protect ourselves. This is, without question, one part of what needs to be done to protect ourselves. But lists by themselves are overwhelming and insufficient.

Relearning a bit of common sense as it applies to our private information is another part of the answer. If we learn what information is valuable and then **change our mindset and habits about how we guard it**, privacy will become second nature and identity thieves will look to easier targets.

Just as we secure our houses using dogs and alarms, lights and locks, we must secure our identities using similar tools. Almost without question, we take steps to secure and protect our precious assets; it is time that we began seeing our identity as one of those assets.

The purpose of this book is not to cause paranoia. Fear is for people who would rather worry than take action. By reading this book, you have already started taking action. My goal is for you to go beyond simply performing a checklist of prevention tasks. Yes, using checklists is an important step, but, by itself, won't protect you over the longer term. Thieves read the same articles that you and I do and will eventually learn to work around those short-term lists. Identity thieves are employed by our apathy—cashing in on our unwillingness to think through the issues and act on our instincts. They prey on inactivity and on those who are unprepared.

This book provides three layers of protection:

1. **Think like a spy.** The first layer of protection is a **Mindset**, or a habitual way of thinking about your private information that will trigger alarms in your head when your identity is at risk. For example, instead of having to remember to shred lists of specific documents, you will develop the habit of destroying any private information that will be handled by others. I call this mindset "think

like a spy." It is based on the idea that to avoid the enemy, we must understand how he or she operates. This, in turn, will allow us to successfully develop habits that protect our long-term privacy. Mindsets are indicated throughout the book using the symbol of a light bulb.

2. **Take action.** The second layer of protection is a series of specific **Action Items** (to-do steps) that should be completed to protect your identity. For example, shred your credit card statements before throwing them away. These Action Items are based on statistical data showing how identities are most commonly stolen and who steals them, not on what hot topic about identity theft is getting the most press coverage at the moment. The Action Items provide the most immediate form of protection and are indicated throughout the book using a checkmark symbol.

3. **Get educated about identity theft.** Throughout the book, I have included statistical data, definitions and methods of identity theft. By accumulating this knowledge, you become aware of how to protect yourself simply using common sense. For example, if one-third of all identity theft occurs because of a lost or stolen wallet, you can begin immediately preventing identity theft by protecting your wallet.

The goal is to make *thinking like a spy* a habit by practicing. I use the Action Items in each chapter to illustrate and reinforce exactly how you start to think like a spy. When you are shredding old bank statements, for example, you aren't just checking an item off your action list. You are reinforcing the habit of destroying anything with a piece of your identity on it that you no longer need.

Then, months down the road, when identity thieves have designed new ways to steal information that isn't covered by anyone's checklist, you will be in the mindset or habit of thinking like a spy. You will automatically destroy unnecessary private information, whether it is a paper bank statement, a compact disc or an expired credit card.

Where prevention isn't possible (because some things are out of our control), my purpose is to minimize the impact of identity theft on our lives. For example, if a business loses your private information (as has happened recently with DSW, ChoicePoint and LexisNexis), you must have a backup plan to help you deal with the fallout. Don't let corporate data loss discourage you from making changes. You are not helpless against this type of identity theft. Giving up would be like refusing to wear a seatbelt because someone might run into you (which is also out of your control). Chapter 10, *Plan B*, is entirely devoted to early theft detection and damage control.

I wish I were able to guarantee that reading and acting on this book would protect you 100%. But it won't. There is no fail-safe against any crime, only ways to better protect ourselves. This book reduces your exposure and vulnerability to identity theft, but is not a cure-all.

It is, however, an attempt to fill a huge void that I encountered in every other book and article I read on identity-theft prevention. We need a call to arms more profound than short-term fear and 10-point checklists:

1. We must make privacy a HABIT, not a one-time checklist.
2. We must understand the ENEMY to protect ourselves.
3. We must learn to THINK critically about our privacy.
4. We must take ACTION in gradual, organized steps.

The crime of identity theft demands that we spend some time thinking about and changing how we share our private information and run our lives. Whether it is a product of this book or another, or whether it's from one of my speaking engagements, word of mouth or by way of the popular media, I hope you will take identity theft seriously **before it happens to you**.

2

Think Like a Spy:
The 7 Mindsets of Prevention

Thinking like a spy is a paradigm designed to help you make a habit of privacy on a daily basis and recognize when your identity is at risk. Stephen Covey describes a paradigm as "a lens through which we see the world."[2] When our identity is involved, we want to view it through the more critical "lens" of a spy.

Why view identity through the eyes of a spy, you ask? **Because for many of us, monitoring our identity through our regular "lenses" isn't working. We don't take significant action when our private information is at risk.** Spies, on the other hand, are trained to have a heightened sense of awareness anytime they are in the field (spying). Learning from this increased level of awareness will significantly help us to prevent identity theft. In its simplest form, thinking like a spy is nothing more than asking yourself:

"What would a spy do if he or she were in my shoes right now?"

Spies don't like to share their information. We must learn to be as critical when *our* personal information is on the table. This does not mean that we need to be paranoid. As our awareness and knowledge increase, fear will decrease. The spy mindset will grow as we actively take steps to protect our privacy and expose less of our identity to danger.

Using espionage as a mindset is meant to be neither perfect nor overly serious, but to give us a common language

Advance knowledge cannot be gained from ghosts and spirits, inferred from phenomena, or projected from the measures of Heaven, but must be gained from men for it is the knowledge of the enemy's true situation.

— Sun Tzu, "Employing Spies" in *The Art of War*

with which to understand and combat identity theft without reinventing the wheel. In fact, my hope is that you will find thinking like a spy entertaining and engaging, and will therefore put it to use. Throughout the book, I use stereotypical spy terms and tactics, not because of their resemblance to reality, but because of their effectiveness in illustrating the **7 Mindsets of Prevention**.

Why Think Like a Spy?

For many people, the thought of thinking like a spy may at first be unattractive. Spies, after all, are devious, dishonest and undesirable characters. And they are the enemy—so much so that we even rename "our" spies "agents" to make them more acceptable.

To defeat our enemies, we must be wise enough to learn from them.

Just as we watch reality TV shows to better understand how real-life burglars operate, we can learn to deter identity thieves by understanding spies.

Why not think like a plain-old identity thief? Because this perspective is limited—it only gives us one-half of the equation, how a thief steals information. For example, by thinking like a thief, we would learn how he or she would steal a wallet. But that does little to educate us on the other half of the equation, how to protect our wallets (other than to suggest that we should never allow our wallet to be stolen, which is impractical).

A spy, on the other hand, operates in both of these worlds—information protection and information collection—simultaneously. Spies go to great lengths and are well trained in *protecting* their real identities, as well as their aliases, informants, sources, agents and entire spy network.

From these skills, we can learn how to protect *our* sensitive information, whether it is physical (paper documents, credit cards, receipts), digital (hard disks, email, internet, ecommerce) or human (what is in our brains). Spies are also masters of *collecting* information (or intelligence) on their subjects. This makes them uniquely qualified to be studied when we our considering our privacy.

A spy *protects* information by applying three simple mindsets:

Simplify. A spy is in the habit of eliminating unnecessary information at the source. For example, most spies are never told the end purpose of their mission, as it adds nothing to their effectiveness and minimizes leaks. Applied to privacy, we can make a habit of eliminating the pieces of our identity that are no longer necessary to our lives. By canceling a credit card that we no longer use, we remove all risk of the card or statements being stolen. We have simplified our identity.

Destroy. A spy makes a habit of destroying any sensitive information that shouldn't be seen by others. For example, when a spy is reporting to his or her superiors, all but one copy of the typed report are burned. Even the typewriter cartridge (in the days of typewriters) was destroyed after use. Applied to identity theft, we should develop the habit of destroying anything with private information that we no longer need. For example, when we are done with a bank statement, we should shred the document.

Secure. Anything that cannot be simplified or destroyed, a spy will lock up or conceal. For example, a spy uses secret codes (like the Enigma machine in *Das Boot*) to protect communication. We can take the same measures with our private information, whether it is by using passwords to protect our computer or safes to protect vital documents.

When you come into contact with a piece of your identity (defined in the next chapter), ask yourself if you want to simplify, destroy or secure the information. Leave yourself no other options.

In addition to the three mindsets above, a spy *collects* information according to four more mindsets. By understanding these mindsets, we will be able to apply them to our advantage—a noble use of counterintelligence:

Accumulate. Spies gather data gradually and methodically, not all at once. Just as a spy collects intelligence over time, we will gather our privacy over time.

Observe & Evaluate. Spies are always observing their surroundings so that they are prepared to make quick, sound decisions. By observing our surroundings when our identity is exposed, we will be prepared to make safe decisions.

Interrogate. Spies ask direct questions to get answers. We will ask questions right back until we are comfortable with their intentions.

Plan B—the backup plan. Spies always have a backup plan, and so must we. We will develop an entirely independent way to monitor our identities in case the other mindsets fail.

Together, these habits of a spy make up the **7 Mindsets of Prevention**.

1ˢᵗ Mindset   Accumulate Privacy

How to approach prevention with minimal time investment and maximum long-term impact (Chapter 4).

2ⁿᵈ Mindset   Simplify Your Identity

How to decrease your exposure by stopping "identity creep" at the source (Chapter 5).

3ʳᵈ Mindset   Destroy Private Information

Which elements of your identity to shred or destroy (Chapter 6).

4ᵗʰ Mindset   Secure the Essentials

Which elements of your identity to lock up or conceal and how to lock them up (Chapter 7).

5ᵗʰ Mindset **Observe & Evaluate**

 Thinking skills to help you monitor your identity and evaluate risk (Chapter 8).

6ᵗʰ Mindset **Interrogate the Enemy**

 How to prevent fraud by asking direct questions of those requesting your identity (Chapter 9).

7ᵗʰ Mindset **Plan B**

 A backup plan for monitoring identity in case the other mindsets don't apply or don't work (Chapter 10).

☑ Action Items: *Think Like a Spy*

To help explain where we are headed, I have listed several examples of how someone might deal with privacy before and after learning to think like a spy. I use these same examples throughout the book and give further explanation. They are based on how a statistically average person (not necessarily you) treats private information. There is a natural overlap, or redundancy, between mindsets, so that privacy can be approached from many directions. The **7 Mindsets of Prevention** appear in **(bold)**.

Situation	Before...	After learning how to think like a spy...
Someone reputable asks for your social security number.	You hesitate, but ultimately justify giving it away, thinking "they can be trusted."	Your identity is "in play," which triggers you to raise your level of awareness **(observe)** and make a judgment about your risk of identity theft **(evaluate)**. Your response is to ask questions until you are comfortable with your safety **(interrogate)**. Chapters 8, 9.

Situation	Before...	After learning how to think like a spy...
A credit card statement arrives in the mail.	You quickly look it over and file it away.	If you are diligent, you make sure that you recognize each transaction.If the statement is from a card that you no longer need or use, you cancel it **(simplify)** and then shred the document **(destroy)**. If it is a necessary piece of identity, you contact the company and request online statements in place of mailed statements (simplify).You review each transaction to make sure they are valid **(Plan B)** and file it in a locked cabinet **(secure)**. Chapters 5, 6, 7, 10.
You sign up for a new credit card.	You take no additional steps.	You opt-out of their information-sharing policy and request that they send you no convenience checks or marketing materials **(simplify)**.You set up online statements instead of paper statements **(secure)**. Chapters 5, 7.
You receive an email from your bank requesting information.	You read it and potentially fill it out since it has your bank's logo and email address on it.	You delete the email and login to your bank account to look for any alerts or notices about the request. If you still have questions, you call the bank **(evaluate)**. Chapter 8.

Situation	Before...	After learning how to think like a spy...
A department store offers a one-time 10% discount if you sign up for their credit card.	If you aren't in a rush and don't already have their card, you accept.	You calculate how much you are earning for your information and decide whether or not it is worth it **(evaluate)**. Chapter 8.
You notice customer data, sensitive intellectual property or employee documents out in the open at work.	You are relieved that you are not the one that is legally liable for the safety of those documents. You clean up your own desk since you know the personal consequences.	You assess the level of risk that the theft of these sensitive documents would cause the business **(evaluate)** and either lock them up **(secure)** or shred them **(destroy)**. You educate your staff on the **7 Mindsets of Prevention** to protect the business's assets, including your employee information. Chapters 6, 7, 8.
You only have a few minutes to protect your identity.	Since one little change won't make a difference anyway, you do nothing.	You figure that one step in the right direction is better than nothing **(accumulation)**. You read Chapter 10, *Plan B* and implement a good backup plan to minimize damage when your identity is stolen. Chapters 4, 10.

Before we can begin thinking like a spy, we need to build the "lens" through which you will view your identity. You must clearly understand what "Identity" is, where it can be found, how you can "accumulate" it, and how it is most vulnerable. That is the subject of the following chapter, *What Is an Identity?*

3

What *Is* an Identity?

Identity is nothing more than how we define ourselves—a mother, wife, piano player, author, etc. But in the realm of privacy and "identity theft," we focus on a subset of identity called **data identity**—which is how others, usually companies, associations or governments, define or reference us. I will refer to data identity simply as *identity* throughout the book.

Identity is made up of any *name, number or attribute* that provides information on us or allows access into further personal data.

Identity is almost always used to link us to money, special privileges or access. For example, our social security number connects us to our retirement and unemployment benefits and tax obligations. Our frequent flyer number gives access to our accrued mileage and membership benefits.

> Give a man a fish
> and you feed him for a day.
> Teach a man to fish and
> you feed him for a lifetime.
>
> Chinese Proverb

Technology has made it easier to replicate these forms of identity. High-resolution scanners and printers have made reproducing licenses, checks and other identity documents a simple affair for identity thieves. As older identity technologies are compromised, newer forms of identity will appear. For example, it won't be long before we are using thumbprints and retinal eye scans to represent ourselves to others. These forms of identity have drawbacks as well, which is why we need to progress beyond simple checklists into habits of privacy that apply to *any* technology.

The Names, Numbers and Attributes of Our Identity

The following is a partial list of the key items that make up our identities. I have left blank spaces for you to include pieces of identity that you think of. **You should not skim this list as it is the foundation**

for the rest of the book. If you don't know what your identity *is*, you won't be able to protect it from thieves.

☐	Full Name	☐	Family member's names
☐	Social security number		and information
☐	Bank account numbers	☐	Photograph
☐	Date of birth	☐	Thumbprint
☐	Address	☐	Retinal pattern
☐	Mother's maiden name	☐	Voice qualities
☐	Computer passwords	☐	DNA
☐	Internet passwords	☐	Height
☐	ATM PINs	☐	Weight
☐	Credit card numbers	☐	Hair Color
☐	Driver's license number	☐	Eye Color
☐	Phone number	☐	Ethnicity
☐	Cell phone number	☐	Nationality
☐	Email address	☐	Sex
☐	Computer IP address	☐	Occupation
☐	Frequent flyer numbers	☐	Income
☐	Garage door opener codes	☐	Religion
☐	Vehicle VIN #	☐	_____

Where Identity Lives –
Paper, Plastic, Human & Electronic

It is equally important to know where these individual pieces of identity can be found. Once you sit down and think about it, the number of places where your identity exists is astounding. Please take the time to indicate the items on the list below that affect you or your family. For example, if you have a driver's license, put a check mark in the box. This checklist will serve as a list of the identity items that you need to protect, and will save you a great deal of time when you reach Chapters 6 and 7, which discuss what information to destroy and what to lock up.

On your person—wallet, purse, briefcase, cell phone, PDA/Palm Pilot

- ☐ Driver's license
- ☐ ID cards (military, student)
- ☐ Social security card
- ☐ Credit cards
- ☐ Debit cards
- ☐ Medical cards
- ☐ Membership cards
- ☐ Business cards
- ☐ Proof of insurance
- ☐ Checks
- ☐ Cell phone
- ☐ Personal Digital Assistants (PDAs)
- ☐ Credit card receipts
- ☐ Address book
- ☐ Passport
- ☐ _____

In your home—mail, desk, filing cabinet, safe, trash

- ☐ Credit card statements
- ☐ Bank statements
- ☐ Credit union statements
- ☐ Brokerage statements
- ☐ Insurance statements
- ☐ Utility statements
- ☐ Mortgage statements
- ☐ Insurance policies
- ☐ Associations and memberships
- ☐ Wills & Trusts
- ☐ Power-of-attorney
- ☐ Living wills
- ☐ Cancelled checks
- ☐ New checks
- ☐ Pay stubs
- ☐ Medical records
- ☐ Tax records
- ☐ Social security statements
- ☐ Birth certificates
- ☐ Passports
- ☐ Mortgage/loan documents
- ☐ Lease and purchase agreements
- ☐ Death certificates
- ☐ Adoption papers
- ☐ Immigration, citizenship papers
- ☐ Marriage license
- ☐ Divorce papers
- ☐ _____

On your computer

- ☐ Contact manager (Outlook)
- ☐ Websites (Banks, Brokers)
- ☐ Google (Reverse lookup)
- ☐ Zabasearch.com
- ☐ Anywho.com
- ☐ Emails
- ☐ On-line bill pay
- ☐ Software (Quicken, Money)
- ☐ CD-ROMS
- ☐ Floppy Disks
- ☐ USB Thumb drives
- ☐ Across wireless networks

At work

- ☐ Personnel records
- ☐ On your computer
- ☐ Identification cards
- ☐ _____

In your car

- ☐ Car registration
- ☐ Proof of insurance
- ☐ Repair receipts
- ☐ _____

In public

- ☐ Government documents (birth certificates, driver's license number, address, real estate owned, SSN, criminal records, property tax rolls, income tax documents, vehicle registration, passport)
- ☐ Licensing entities (fishing, hunting, driver's, marriage)
- ☐ Property deeds & records

In data warehouses & businesses—Businesses keep records on us to sell to other businesses for marketing purposes or to market directly to us:

- ☐ ChoicePoint
- ☐ Seisint
- ☐ Lexis/Nexis
- ☐ Equifax
- ☐ TransUnion
- ☐ Experian
- ☐ Retail stores (DSW, Walmart, etc.)
- ☐ Credit card companies
- ☐ Reunion websites
- ☐ "Find a friend" websites

IN OUR BRAINS! —We store much of this information in our heads and share it through our mouths.

The Most Common Forms of Identity Theft

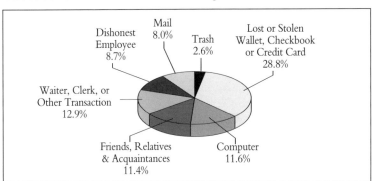

Source: Javelin Strategy Research & The Better Business Bureau – The 2005 Identity Fraud Survey

It is important to be familiar with these categories of theft because it already *gives you a view of how to protect yourself.* Watch your risk go down as you take steps to protect yourself:

Preventative Step		Your Risk Is:
	For the sake of this exercise, assume that you start with a 100% chance of having your identity stolen	100%
	Keep from having your wallet lost or stolen OR take steps to protect your identity in case it is stolen (Chapter 5, *Simplify your Identity*).	71%
	Protect your PC from viruses, anti-spyware, hackers and thieves (Chapter 7, *Secure the Essentials*).	60%
	Don't leave pieces of identity lying around for dishonest friends, family and guests to steal (Chapter 6, *Destroy Private Information* and Chapter 7, *Secure the Essentials*).	49%

Preventative Step	Your Risk Is:
Know how to prevent identity theft in restaurants, retail stores and any other time your credit card goes out of your sight (Chapter 8, *Observe & Evaluate*).	39%
Don't leave pieces of identity lying around at work for dishonest co-workers, customers or building staff to steal (Chapter 6, *Destroy Private Information* and Chapter 7, *Secure the Essentials*).	30%
Protect incoming and outgoing mail (Chapter 7, *Secure the Essentials*).	22%
Shred documents that would otherwise go out in the trash (Chapter 6, *Destroy Private Information*).	19%
Learn how to accumulate privacy beyond checklists. Learn to think critically about what information you share with others. Know how to recognize a fraud, what questions to ask to be certain and how to protect yourself with a backup plan (Chapters 4, *Accumulate Privacy*, Chapter 8, *Observe & Evaluate*, Chapter 9, *Interrogate the Enemy* and Chapter 10, *Plan B*).	9%★★

★★I estimate that the "thinking" chapters of this book will lower your chances by at least an additional 10%. This would bring your chances of being a victim of identity theft down to 9%. But that is based on having a 100% chance of identity theft, which you don't. You actually have about a 5% chance of identity theft every year, which means that after taking these precautions, you should reduce your chances to **less than 1% per year**, even if you fail to implement some of the steps in the book. Those are much better odds!

Who Steals Identities?

Remarkably, in a recent survey, of the people who knew how their identity had been stolen, **50% of them said they knew the thief.**

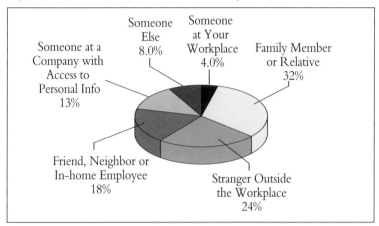

Someone Else
8.0%

Someone at Your Workplace
4.0%

Family Member or Relative
32%

Someone at a Company with Access to Personal Info
13%

Friend, Neighbor or In-home Employee
18%

Stranger Outside the Workplace
24%

Source: Javelin Strategy Research & The Better Business Bureau – The 2005 Identity Fraud Survey

You certainly can't avoid all of these people, but you can be more careful with your identity around them. It is easier to make a blanket rule, i.e., don't allow anyone access to your identity unless it is absolutely necessary, than to make exceptions. This includes family members (generally other than spouses) and friends. If you let them know that you don't give this information out to **anyone**, they shouldn't be offended.

The Trigger—Your First Reaction to Sharing Identity

The trigger, or what causes you to be on high alert, is actually very simple—it is the appearance of your identity in any form (wallet, credit card, tax form, passport, driver's license, etc).

Anytime someone requests or has access to any of the names, numbers or attributes that define your identity, or to the paper, plastic, digital or human data where your identity lives, an alarm should sound in your head.

You should regard this person or situation as a risk to your identity until proven innocent. When your identity is being shared in any way, it should trigger you to ask yourself:

> *Is the risk of giving this piece of identity away in this specific situation worth the benefit?*

It is at this point that you use the 7 Mindsets of Prevention to determine whether or not to share your information.

If, for example, you are visiting a music website that requests some of your personal information in exchange for songs, you should:

1. **Stop.**

2. **Evaluate** the risk (giving away identity) vs. the reward (songs).

3. **Consider the consequences.** For example, if they are requesting your name and email address, what could they do with that information? They could sell it to spam marketers, set up accounts on distasteful websites in your name, use your email as the return address on spam, etc.

Chances are good that this won't be the case, especially if it is a reputable site. But you need to go through the process with each website so that you develop the habit. When you are willing to exchange your information for a benefit, make sure that you read their privacy disclosure policies and opt-out of information sharing. This will be discussed in detail in Chapter 5, *Simplify your Identity*.

The next chapter, *Accumulate Privacy*, is the first of the 7 Mindsets of Prevention.

4

The 1st Mindset— Accumulate Privacy, One Step at a Time

Spies are patient. They collect small, seemingly meaningless pieces of information until it adds up to a goldmine.

Stolen Life #462

One day at the gym, an identity thief was watching over Michelle's shoulder while she dialed the **combination** *on her locker. Having observed her habits for several weeks, the thief knew that she drove a nice car and that she exercised three times a week after work for approximately an hour.*

The following week, just after leaving the locker room to work out, the thief broke into Michelle's locker and stole her **wallet.** *While in her locker, the thief noted her cell-phone* **number.** *When she returned from working out, she discovered that her wallet was gone. She walked to her car to make sure she hadn't left it there, and as she was unlocking the car, she received a call on her cell phone.*

> ———
> *Little strokes fell great oaks.*
>
> — Benjamin Franklin,
> *Poor Richard's Almanac*
> ———

It was her bank saying that they had caught someone trying to use her cards to obtain cash. The security guard had stopped the thief, taken her into custody and needed Michelle to positively identify the contents of her wallet. For security purposes, they asked Michelle to verify her **account information,** *including* **social security number** *and* **mother's maiden name.** *They suggested that she immediately change her PIN number with them on the phone before any further damage was done. In a panic, Michelle gave them the information, including her existing* **PIN number.**

The bank caller, actually part of an identity theft ring, had just "socially engineered" (conned) her into giving away even more damaging information by establishing a relationship of trust using the pieces of information they had collected in her locker.

*By systematically collecting her identity, they drained her **bank account**, charged thousands of dollars to her **credit cards**, set up "official" **driver's licenses** with her information (and other people's pictures), used the licenses to steal six rental cars, and purchase plane tickets to fly across the country under her name. Her identity was sold on the internet for use by other thieves who will probably never be caught.*

Within months, Michelle had warrants for her arrest in several states and is still battling multiple identities across the country. And because there is currently no federal jurisdiction over identity theft, Michelle has to fight the battle mostly alone, one local jurisdiction at a time.

Just as identity thieves have learned to collect data with the patience of spies, we must learn how to gradually safeguard our privacy using the same mindset. We must **accumulate privacy** and we must **accumulate knowledge** about how identity thieves operate!

Most Americans secure pieces of their identity, but not all of their identity. This would be similar to locking your front door, but not your back. By developing habits of privacy instead of acting out of panic, you will make far more progress over time.

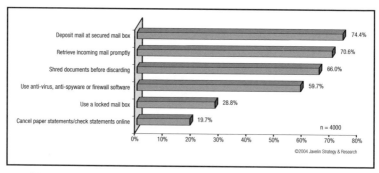

QA "Which of the following activities do you conduct regularly?"

Spy Mindset: To avoid detection, spies collect sensitive information in small, unnoticeable pieces over a period of time.

<u>Accumulate</u> Mindset: We will learn to gather or accumulate privacy over time by taking small, organized steps. By making privacy a habit, we stop the slow leakage of our information and greatly reduce our chances of becoming victims of identity theft.

Think about it…slowly, over time, we have given away our privacy. Many times we don't even realize we are giving it away. We commonly trade our personal information for access to website content (free songs, email), the chance to win a contest (iPods, vacations) or a one-time 10% discount

> —
> *True life is lived when tiny changes occur.*
> — Leo Tolstoy
> —

at a clothing retailer. I call this slow and unnecessary leakage of our personal information *identity creep,* and the people who collect our information to use it for their own gain *identity creeps* (also referred to throughout the book as spies and thieves). Our information is requested in a subtle way, and because the immediate benefits seem substantial and often feel harmless, we overlook the downside—that we are gradually broadcasting our identity to those who shouldn't have it.

Now is the time to stop identity creep!

One source at a time, we must reverse our bad habits and guard information rather than give it out. Understandably, we cannot entirely give up sharing our information. But we must determine what to share and with whom—and that is where thinking like a spy can help.

By adopting a mindset of accumulation, you will begin regaining your privacy immediately and one step at a time. This incremental approach keeps prevention from being an overwhelming task and reminds you to consider the risk anytime identity is involved.

Because of the power of accumulation, you can spend just minutes a day taking steps toward protecting your privacy and still make substantial progress over time.

Prevention is not a one-time fix. I discourage you from sitting down one weekend to attain privacy. Done in this way, the task will overwhelm even the most diligent worker-bee. You need to accumulate small pieces of change over many months to protect yourself in an enduring and effective way. Think about accumulating privacy as Benjamin Franklin did about saving money—put a little away every chance you get and before long, you will have amassed a fortune.

The example below demonstrates the habit of accumulating privacy versus making it a one-time project (which is how it is often presented in books, articles and speeches). The mindset of accumulation is a particular *way* of implementing all of the remaining mindsets. For example, you should get in the habit of simplifying, destroying or securing private information as you come into daily contact with it, not when it piles up. The mindsets that will help you protect your identity in each case appear in **(bold parentheses)**.

An Example of Accumulation–Protecting Your Mail

You see a news story about identity thieves stealing mail from unlocked mailboxes outside of people's houses. You never realized how much money could be stolen from the mail. The thieves "wash" checks and place their name in the "Pay To" field, use credit card numbers to buy items on the internet and apply for bank loans with your Social Security number. You learn that because your mailbox has no lock, your chances of having mail stolen are much higher. The news story suggests that you pick up your mail shortly after it is delivered and mail outgoing items from a USPS box.

The One-time Method: For the next couple of weeks, operating purely out of fear, you pick up your mail a few hours after it is delivered. In addition, you drop your outgoing mail in the USPS box at your local supermarket. Over time, because your mail isn't stolen and the news story is forgotten, you let your guard down. The short-term fear is gone and so is your motivation to protect your identity. You go back to your old habit—picking up your mail when it is convenient and mailing outgoing mail from the unlocked box. You are right back where you started.

Accumulation Mindset: Realizing that you can't realistically make it home every day within an hour or two of mail delivery, you take a longer-term approach of protecting your mail and make a *new habit* out of it. You break the job down into small, manageable steps (like those listed in Chapter 12, *Your Calendar of Prevention*). You implement these items over the course of a few months **(Accumulate Privacy)**.

Day 1: You receive a statement for a credit card that you no longer use. You call the credit card company and cancel the card **(Simplify)**. You shred the statement, because you no longer need it **(Destroy)**. In 10 minutes, you have eliminated this piece of mail completely.

Day 7: You receive several pieces of junk mail. You log on to the Direct Marketing Association website and remove yourself from their junk mail list **(Simplify)**. From today forward, you will spend far less time opening junk mail. On future days you will remove yourself from further lists, but you have completed your task for today **(Accumulate Privacy)**.

Day 9: You need to pay your phone bill. Instead of sending a check through the mail, you call and set up a recurring automatic payment on your credit card **(Simplify)**. You earn mileage points every month by putting it on your credit card and have an easy way to dispute charges if necessary (the credit card company does it for you). While you are on with the phone company, you ask them to stop mailing you paper statements and request that all correspondence be sent by email **(Simplify)**. You have eliminated another piece of mail and another source of risk.

Day 14: You receive a statement for a credit card that you use constantly. With the statement, you receive "courtesy" or "convenience" checks that usually have a 20% interest rate. You contact the credit card company and ask them to send you online statements only, which eliminates a third piece of mail and another place for your identity to be stolen **(Simplify)**. While you have them on the phone, you opt out of information sharing (when they sell your data) and request that you no longer receive courtesy or convenience checks, which are a favorite of identity thieves **(Simplify)**. You shred the "courtesy checks" **(Destroy)**, review your statement for any charges that you didn't make **(Plan B)** and file the statement in a locking filing cabinet **(Secure)**.

In this example, you have already eliminated 36 separate pieces of mail that could have been stolen this year (3 statements for 12 months each). By day sixty, you will have completed two cycles of mail and will have eliminated or cancelled a majority of what can be stolen. Even if you only eliminate 30 total documents, this translates into removing 360 pieces of mail a year, or one piece of susceptible identity per day. That significantly lowers the odds that an identity thief will find a useful document in your mail.

Congratulations! You have started to accumulate privacy.

This same mindset can be applied to numerous areas: opening new accounts, entering contests, protecting your computer, answering telemarketing calls, educating yourself about identity theft, and so on. These are discussed throughout the book.

☑ Action Items: Accumulate Knowledge about Identity Thieves

In addition to accumulating privacy, it is important to begin accumulating a background in how identity thieves work. What methods do they use? Where are you vulnerable? The more you know about their methods, the louder the alarms will ring when you encounter one of these situations. The following list gives some of the methods that identity thieves commonly use. The mindset that will help you combat the particular method is listed in **(bold)**:

- **Dumpster Diving:** This is when a spy (or thief) rummages through your home or business garbage looking for documents that allow them to set up new credit card accounts, establish phone service, open bank accounts, take out loans, etc. **(Destroy)**.

- **Shoulder Surfing:** This happens when a spy peers over your shoulder at an ATM machine or grocery store to obtain your PIN number. Sometimes they use hidden cameras and cell-phone cameras **(Observe & Evaluate)**.

- **Corporate Data Loss:** This happens when a major business loses your private information (as happened recently with Bank of America). Sometimes it is stolen by one of the other methods **(Plan B)**.

- **Social Engineering:** This occurs when a spy uses our human tendencies to trust others and avoid confrontation to coax information out of us **(Observe & Evaluate; Interrogate)**.

- **Red-Flagging:** This is when a spy steals the mail from your home or business mailbox, usually to apply for pre-approved credit cards, intercept new credit and debit cards and to steal your new checks. Putting up the red flag on your mailbox signals identity thieves that you have something worth stealing **(Secure)**.

- **Midnight Mailing:** This is when a spy cuts a hole in the bottom of blue USPS mailboxes and regularly picks up mail, generally to "wash" checks. Many times, they just steal the entire box in the middle of the night and replace it by morning **(Secure)**.

- **Computer Hacking:** This happens when a spy uses spyware, viruses or hacking tools to get at the information on your computer— usually passwords, credit card numbers and bank accounts **(Secure)**.

- **Old-fashioned Stealing:** This occurs when a spy steals or finds your lost wallet, purse, checkbook, credit card, driver's license, passport, etc. This also applies to credit card receipts and checks left on restaurant tables **(Simplify; Observe & Evaluate)**.

- **Skimming:** Occurs when a spy (waiter, retail clerk, etc.) legitimately processes your credit card and then swipes it through a hand-held "skimmer" to be used for credit card fraud **(Observe & Evaluate; Plan B)**.

- **ATM Skimming:** When a spy installs a "skimmer" on an ATM machine to capture your card number, expiration date, name, etc. Coupled with shoulder surfing (or a hidden camera), this gives a spy everything needed to drain your bank account **(Observe & Evaluate)**.

- **ID Shoplifting:** This is when a friend, family member, contract laborer or domestic help (spy) takes identity documents out of your home or business (or copies down information and leaves the materials). These are the most difficult crimes to catch, and they carry the highest price tag. These types of thieves often use this information to file bankruptcy, take out a car loan, pay drug or gambling debts or present an alternate identity if they are arrested (**Destroy & Secure**).

- **Phishing:** Occurs when a spy sends you an email that appears to be from a familiar source, such as your bank, PayPal, eBay, your brokerage, etc. The spy asks you to fill out a form with your personal information and uses it to break into your real account (**Observe & Evaluate**).

- **Pharming:** This is when computer hackers temporarily take over website addresses to make you think you are at your bank or other financial institution when you are really entering information on the hacker's data collection site. They use this data to break into your real account. How they do this is less important than how to protect yourself (**Plan B**).

- **War Driving:** This is when a spy drives around neighborhoods looking for unprotected wireless networks. When discovered, he or she uses your internet connection to commit crimes (usually associated with pornography or methamphetamines) or to browse your computer and steal information (**Secure**).

- **Evil Twinning:** This is when a spy sets up an identical wireless network at your favorite wireless hot-spot (e.g., an internet café). When you log on to the network, the hacker is able to browse your computer and steal data (**Secure**).

 Identity theft is more costly to you when information is obtained by conventional methods (e.g., the thief steals your wallet or checkbook) than by electronic methods (hackers, viruses, phishing emails, etc.).

The average (mean) cost to victims by type of theft:

Phishing Emails:	**$2,320**
Theft of Paper Mail:	**$9,243**
Family, Friends & others:	**$15,607**

5

The 2nd Mindset—
Simplify Your Identity

Identity thieves target wallets and purses because they contain such a high concentration of private information. The average purse contains over 20 pieces of identity (name, phone number, credit card numbers, etc.).

Stolen Life #891

Sherri lived out of her purse. Because she often traveled while on the job, she carried everything she would possibly need on the road—her passport, several credit cards, Palm Pilot, medical cards, Social Security card, her parent's vital information, and more. When she was in her office, Sherri tucked her purse safely in the desk drawer. Most of her female coworkers just left them sitting under their desks.

Someone must have been spying on her because her wallet and Palm Pilot disappeared out of the purse while her group was in a 9 a.m. weekly meeting that lasted only fifteen minutes. She didn't discover they were missing for almost three hours when she grabbed her purse to go to lunch. Sherri had so many credit cards and pieces of identity in her wallet that she couldn't possibly remember all of her accounts on short notice. She was unable to quickly lock down her identity.

Within hours, Sherri's credit cards had already been maxed out. They had been used to buy several cell phones, two bottles of hard alcohol, two semi-automatic pistols and 500 rounds of ammunition. By the second day, someone had applied for credit in her name as well as her father's name (his information was in the Palm Pilot). The issuer of a debit card had granted the thief a line of credit and honored it even with a growing negative balance. Overdraft protection, the bank called it, ironically.

Sherri eventually learned that there was a petty theft robbery charge against her in another state. Someone who had purchased her stolen identity off of the internet was caught shoplifting and gave the police Sherri's name, date of birth and driver's license. The State Patrol arrested the thief later for another offense and while running a check, spotted the ID theft. Had it not been for that discovery, Sherri wouldn't have known "she" had a date to appear in criminal court and a warrant would have been issued for her arrest.

Sherri's purse is now much lighter—she carries only a driver's license and one credit card. When she travels, she keeps her documents in a necklace purse. When she is in the office, she always locks her purse in a filing cabinet.

It is impractical to think that we can keep our wallets and purses from ever being lost or stolen. To protect our identities, therefore, we need to reduce identity exposure in our wallets, purses, homes and cars. We do this by **Simplifying Our Identities!**

"Lost or stolen wallets, purses or checkbooks is the number one known identity fraud access method."

— *The 2005 Identity Fraud Survey Report,*
Javelin Strategy & Research

 Spy Mindset: To protect themselves, spies carry very little incriminating information with them. In addition, they know as little sensitive information as possible about their mission. That way, if they fall into the hands of the enemy, they have little to share.

Simplify Mindset: The fewer pieces of private information we carry with us (in wallets, purses, PDAs, etc.), the less damage we will sustain if they are lost or stolen. Simplifying our Identity prepares us for the worst-case scenario.

Spy networks operate on a need-to-know-basis. Spies are told no more than necessary, carry no more than necessary, and talk no more than necessary. Information is simplified because it is easier to track and keep safe. In addition, spies travel light. They carry no "incriminating" documents with them unless absolutely necessary.

The same should be true of your identity. The fewer pieces of personal information rattling around in your wallet, computer, filing cabinet and brain (e.g., credit cards, bank accounts, brokerages, ID cards, passwords, etc.), the lower your statistical risk of loss or theft. The mindset of **simplification** suggests that if you don't need a particular piece of identity, get rid of it *at the source.* The source is whoever or whatever is generating the sensitive document.

This is a three-step accumulation process:

1. Over the course of the next month, cancel every piece of plastic, paper and electronic identity that you no longer use or need.

I do believe in simplicity. When the mathematician would solve a difficult problem, he first frees the equation from all encumbrances, and reduces it to its simplest terms. So simplify the problem of life, distinguish the necessary and the real.

— Henry David Thoreau, *Walden Pond*

2. Be more honest with yourself and *cancel more* (i.e., recognize that you are the product of highly-researched target marketing and you don't actually need a credit card just because it has your favorite NFL team on it).

3. Stop signing up for new accounts unless they are absolutely necessary.

By keeping our identities simple and sharing them on a need-to-know basis, we have less to lose, less to be stolen, less to shred, less to lock up, and more time and brain cells to protect items that are actually necessary.

✔️ Action Items: Simplify Your Identity

Protect Your Wallet and/or Purse

A lost or stolen wallet, purse, checkbook or credit card accounts for 29% of identity theft[4]. That means we can prevent a pretty large piece of the identity theft pie if we simply protect our wallets. But this isn't always possible, so we must minimize damage if it does fall into the wrong hands. The fewer pieces of identity you have in your wallet, the less susceptible you are to theft and the easier it is to recover if you suddenly become a victim. Just as a spy prepares himself in case he falls into the hands of the enemy, you should be prepared for your wallet or purse to end up in the hands of a thief.

First, remove the following items from your wallet or purse:

☐ **Social Security Card.** You only need this in rare circumstances (e.g., your first day on the job). If stolen, it can be used to set up new credit card accounts, driver's licenses, loans and bank accounts. It can also be used to steal your retirement benefits, draw unemployment or file for bankruptcy. Your Social Security number is one piece of your identity that you should protect fiercely. File your card in a fire-safe as discussed in *Securing the Essentials*.

☐ **Checks.** Check fraud is one of the largest and easiest forms of identity theft. Stop carrying checks and use your credit card, debit card or cash. If you can't survive without checks, carry them only when you go shopping, and make sure that your account has as little in it as possible (transfer any excess into your savings until you need it). Don't make excuses for skipping this task—it could have very negative consequences.

• Carrying only one check in your purse or wallet isn't going to help much. It is not just the physical check that the thief is looking for, but the account and bank routing numbers on the bottom of the check that allow the thief to make duplicate checks or access the account electronically.

• Make sure that you don't have your SSN, driver's license number or home telephone number on your checks. It is preferable to use a work address and phone number, which doesn't lead back to your home. Some people advise that you have your first and middle initial printed on the check instead of your full name. This does a good job of concealing your name, but most banks don't verify signatures on checks less than $3,000 anyway, so it probably won't stop fraud.

• Never put full account numbers or Social Security numbers on the Notes line of your check. Use the lasts four digits only—banks and credit card companies can identify you from these numbers.

• Make sure to always sign your checks (and vital documents) with a felt-tip or pigmented ink-pen (like a uni-ball® 207™ gel pen) or permanent marker (like a Sharpie®). This helps prevent thieves from "lifting" the ink from checks, mortgages and other vital documents.

☐ **PIN Numbers and Passwords.** Remove all passwords and PIN numbers from your purse or wallet for bank accounts, websites, debit cards, computers, home alarms, garage doors, etc. See Chapter 7, *Secure the Essentials,* for an easy way to create and remember passwords so that you won't have to carry them with you.

☐ **Excess Credit and Debit Cards.** We tend to collect credit cards and bank accounts even though we don't need them (usually because we received a short-term bribe for signing up). Remove them from your wallet and then cancel all of these accounts. If possible, carry no more than two cards in your wallet. This makes post-theft recovery much easier and less time-consuming.

☐ **Credit Card Receipts.** File them securely if you need them for tax purposes or expense tracking. Otherwise, destroy them. To learn about how best to destroy documents, credit cards, CD-ROMs, and other forms of identity, go to Chapter 6, *Destroy Private Information.* You will find more information on what to lock up and how to secure your documents when you read Chapter 7, *Secure the Essentials.*

☐ **ATM Receipts and Bank Deposit Slips.** Record the transactions and shred them once they have cleared your bank.

Second, have your Social Security number (SSN) removed from any identification cards:

☐ **Driver's License.** In many states, SSNs appear on your driver's license. Most states will allow you to keep it off your card, but it may require getting a new driver's license. It is worth the trouble.

☐ **Medical Cards.** SSNs are often printed on medical insurance or HMO/PPO cards. In many states, the insurance company is required to send you a new card with a non-SSN identification number if requested. Make the request.

☐ **Student ID Cards.** Many colleges and universities use your SSN as a student ID number. Request a new card with a different method of identification.

☐ **Military ID/Government Cards.** Many government-issued cards use your SSN for identification. Some branches of the military require you to carry your card at all times, in which case you are out of luck. Check with your specific agency or branch to find out if you must carry your card at all times. Otherwise, carry it only when necessary.

Third, take precautions in case your wallet is stolen:

☐ **Signature & "Photo ID Required."** Sign your credit cards with *both your signature and "Photo ID Required."* Also, write the same message on the front of the card with indelible ink (since most stores don't even look at your signature on the back). It can be removed somewhat easily, but it helps discourage thieves as they know you are watching out for identity theft.

Please be aware that you need to sign your name on the back of the card to be in compliance with many credit card company contracts. Without your signature, some of them are able to deny any claims of fraud and refuse to reimburse what was stolen. **Don't simply put "Photo ID Required."**

☐ **Photocopy.** Make a photocopy (front and back) of every piece of identity that stays in your wallet. If it is lost or stolen, this will make it easy to call the companies and cancel your cards, accounts, etc. File it in your dossier, discussed in *Plan B*.

From today on, make your wallet a sacred place. Don't add information to it unless it is absolutely necessary. Use it as a control point to stop identity creep. Lock it up at the gym (in private) and don't leave it exposed in your car or at work.

Here are two additional steps I suggest you take:

☐ **Rotate your Credit Cards.** If you have been a victim of data loss (where your private data is lost or stolen from a major corporation as happened recently with DSW, ChoicePoint, LexisNexis, etc.) or just want to "outdate" your credit card identity, once a year cancel the cards you do keep. Call each credit card company, cancel your existing card and have them issue a new card with a new credit card number. This means that all of those companies that have your credit card on file now have old data. And now that you have opted out of a great deal of information sharing, your new card number won't be in as many databases.

• Make sure you have any frequent flyer miles transferred to your new card number, or have your frequent flyer number attached to the new card. You don't want to lose miles just because you are being diligent.

• Don't forget to call any companies that have your credit card number on file for auto-pay (AOL, phone bill, electricity, etc.) and let them know your new number. Anyone who tries to use the old number will draw blanks. This measure isn't to protect against money loss (you only have a $50 liability on any credit card if you report it as lost or stolen in their "acceptable" time frame). It's to protect against having to spend extra time if your credit card number is stolen.

☐ **Pay with Cash.** This old-fashioned way of paying has absolutely *zero identity creep*. Pay with cash when you don't want to let your card out of your sight or don't want to share information that will ultimately be stored in a database and sold to other businesses. Companies buy your credit card histories so they can market other services to you. For example, certain businesses know that if you shop at a particular store, you are likely to buy their product.

Don't forget to have your spouse or partner follow the same steps.

Opt-Out of Information Sharing, Telemarketing and Junk Mail

Your personal information is collected, sold and resold. It is generally used to determine credit risk and marketing departments use it to sell items to you. As you learn of companies and organizations that collect your data, **OPT-OUT** of their information sharing. You opt-out by calling the number on your statement or card and asking them about their privacy policy. If they are speaking in legal gibberish, tell them that you don't want your personal information to be shared with anyone (including other subsidiaries of the same company). Ask to be removed from all junk mail and marketing lists, telemarketing lists and any other form of marketing. Ask that they no longer send "convenience checks," "courtesy checks," pre-approved credit cards or any other form of credit.

As you start to go undercover, you will be reducing the quantity of information you share within and between companies. This lowers your chances of identity theft, and saves you time opening and shredding useless mail.

Here are a handful of places to opt-out. Contact one or two a day for a few weeks and you will start to see your junk mail and telemarketing calls diminish. Alternatively, follow *Your Calendar of Prevention* and you will have opted out of these lists after only a month.

Many of the "opt-out" addresses change frequently (maybe so that people have a harder time opting out). The opt-out links are printed below, but if the links are no longer working, or you would like a centralized place for all opt-out websites, please visit *www.thinklikeaspy.com*.

☐ **Credit Cards.** For each credit card that you haven't cancelled, contact the issuer and tell them that you wish to opt-out of all information sharing, both within their company and with other companies.

• While you have them on the phone, ask them to stop sending you convenience checks (which are frequently stolen from mail boxes), marketing emails and telemarketing calls. Ask them whom else you need to contact within the company to get off *all* lists.

• Finally, ask them if you can receive your statements by email only, as these are another item routinely stolen out of unlocked mail boxes. The benefits of online statements will be discussed in *Securing the Essentials*.

If you aren't comfortable using a computer to receive statements, or don't have a computer, you will learn in Chapter 7, *Secure the Essentials,* how to protect your mail. It is important to make the 7 Mindsets of Prevention work within your lifestyle as that is the only practical way that you will follow through on the changes.

☐ **Financial Institutions.** Contact your insurance companies, brokerages, banks and any other financial institutions and opt-out of all information sharing. Move to online statements where possible. As statements arrive for each of these institutions, make the changes.

☐ **Credit Offers.** Opt-out of pre-screened credit offers, which are frequently stolen from mailboxes. Pre-screened credit offers are when companies check your credit history with one of the three credit bureaus (Equifax, Experian or TransUnion) prior to sending you an offer for more credit based on your good history. This could be a pre-approved credit card, loan or line of credit, etc. Call 1-888-5OPTOUT (1-888-567-8688) or visit *www.optoutprescreen.com*. Because the credit is pre-approved, it is a very attractive target for an identity thief.

☐ **Telemarketing.** Place your name on the National Do Not Call Registry. This will cut down considerably on telemarketing calls. Visit *www.donotcall.gov* and fill out the form for adding your phone numbers (home, cell, business, spouse's cell).

☐ **Telemarketing.** Also place your name on the State Do Not Call Registry, if your state has one. For my home state—Colorado—you can find it at *www.coloradonocall.com* or call 1-888-249-9097. Don't forget to add any home phone numbers as well as cell phones, business phones and your spouse's or partner's cell phone. For a list of other states, please visit our website.

☐ **Junk Mail.** Remove your name from the Direct Marketing Association's mailing list. This will cut down on junk mail. Visit *www.dmaconsumers.org/cgi/offmailinglistdave* and fill out the form for removing your name. It costs $5 if you want to register online (which stops mail more quickly) or it's free if you mail it in. Don't forget to remove your spouse's name as well.

• While at this site, also remove your name from the Direct Marketing Association's telemarketing list. This will eliminate more telemarketing calls (even if you are on a state or national Do-Not-Call List). Visit *www.dmaconsumers.org/cgi/offtelephone* and fill out the form for removing your name. Like the mailing list, it costs $5 if you want to register online. Don't forget to remove your spouse as well.

Tip: If you are registering on both lists for you and your spouse or partner, print out the forms and send them all at once (instead of registering online). This will save you $20. It will take a little longer to get your name off of the lists, but it will save you money.

☐ **Junk Mail.** Here are four additional companies that sell mailing lists that you will want to contact (and more companies are being created every year to gather and market your information). You will need to contact them by mail. Make up a form letter that includes your name and address, phone number and email address. Request that you be removed from all of their mailing lists. Tell them that you want to opt out of all information sharing. The four companies you currently need to contact are:

• Database America, Compilation Department, 470 Chestnut Road, Woodcliff, NJ 07677

• Dun & Bradstreet, Customer Service, 899 Eaton Ave., Bethlehem, PA 18025

• Metromail Corporation, List Maintenance, 901 W. Bond, Lincoln, NE 68521

• R.L. Polk & Co., Name Deletion File, List Compilation Department, 26955 Northwestern Hwy, Southfield, MI 48034-4716

☐ **Directories.** Remove your phone number from Google's reverse directory. To see if your number is listed, go to *www.google.com* and type your phone number into the search window. If it comes up with your name or address, you're listed! Visit *www.google.com/ help/pbremoval.html* and fill out the form to have your information removed.

☐ **Directories.** Remove your personal information from Zabasearch. To see if your personal information is listed, go to *www.zabasearch.com* and type your name into the search window. If it comes up with your name or address, you're listed! Email *info@zabasearch.com* with your full name and address to have your information removed. They will mail you back with a list of options that can be taken.

There are many websites like Zabasearch that aggregate data and offer it for sale. Other examples are *anywho.com, anybirthday.com, completedetective.com* and *findsomeone.com.* The key is to remove your name from each search engine as you hear about them. To do this, simply test to see if your information is in their database (as you did above) and email them to have it removed. In many cases they will require you to mail the request (which discourages people from doing it). Make sure you mail safely. Request that they send you a confirmation of removal so that you can hold them accountable if necessary.

☐ **Directories.** Call your local phone company and ask them to unlist your phone number when the next White Pages is published. This is where many mailing list companies collect data and sell it to other companies.

☐ **Junk Mail.** To stop receiving many catalogs, email *optout@abacus-direct.com* and request that you be taken off of their lists. Include your full name and address, and the name of your spouse or partner as well.

☐ **Junk Mail.** Opt-out of marketing lists generated from public county property records. Visit *www.acxiom.com* and click on the Contact Us link. Once you are on the Contact Us page, use the drop-down menu that says Select a Subject to go to **U.S. Consumer Opt Out**. This allows you to request an opt-out form, which they will only send to you through the mail.

☐ **Discounts and Contests.** Learn to say "No." Stop signing up for new credit cards, checking accounts, contests, discount cards, even if the bribe is appealing. The amount of time that you will save by keeping your identity more private and by eliminating hours opening junk mail will more than surpass the bribe you were being offered.

☐ **Warranty Cards.** Stop filling out Warranty Registration Cards unless it is necessary to enact the warranty (it rarely is). These cards are generally used by the marketing department of companies that want to sell your information to other businesses or sell you related items. They often request a great deal of personal information that has nothing to do with warranties.

☐ **Surveys**. Stop completing surveys unless they are anonymous or very important to you. Check the back of "anonymous" surveys for a small barcode that links the survey to your identity.

Reduce Incoming Mail

The more mail you stop, junk or legitimate, the less chance it will be stolen. Mail theft is easy and very productive for identity thieves, especially when you don't have a locking box. Using mail as a reminder to simplify your identity is an excellent way to accumulate change—as long as you act on the items as they arrive in the mail.

☐ **Online Statements.** Every time a piece of legitimate mail (credit card, bank, insurance, telephone, energy, water and sewage statements, mileage points, etc.) arrives over the next few months, call the company using the customer service number on the statement and ask to receive your statement online. Review and store your statements on your computer if possible. It will be much safer there (especially once you have read *Securing the Essentials*) than receiving them through the mail and storing them in a file cabinet. If you don't use a computer, read the section on securing your mail in *Securing the Essentials*.

☐ **Simplify your mail.** Ask yourself how much you use the account and if you absolutely need it. If you no longer use the account, cancel it, just like you did for your wallet items in *Simplifying your Identity*. If you miss one, catch it next month. This is the beauty of accumulation; it doesn't all have to be done today.

Protect your PDA (Personal Digital Assistant) and Cell Phone

PDAs carry a treasure trove of information, whether they are integrated with your cell phone or independent (like a Palm Pilot). They often have passwords, Social Security numbers, bank account numbers, birth dates, addresses and phone numbers stored in them (for you and all of your contacts). Most people don't choose to turn on password protection on their phones and PDAs.

☐ **Passwords.** Most PDAs have password protection. This tends to work well on independent devices like Palm Pilots, but not so well on phones (some of them have a tendency to lock up in mid-usage if you require a password). If you can password protect the contact management functions only (not the whole use of the phone), it seems to work better. Password protection on devices like these is quickly becoming more sophisticated, so check your cell phone or PDA manual for details.

☐ If you can't lock your phone, use the password suggestions in *Secure the Essentials* to conceal your passwords and private information.

☐ Take private information out of the PDA if you have no way to protect the data.

Reduce Unnecessary Internet Accounts and Website Access

☐ When you are on an internet site that will give you free content in exchange for your personal information (like newspapers, music downloads and web-support) think twice about making the trade. Is the content really worth it? If so, provide as little data as required to get the benefit, and see if it will accept generic data (John Doe, 123 Main St…). If you want to avoid further spam, give a fake email address like *abc@def.com*. If they require a confirmation email (one you have to open and respond to) you will need to give them a legitimate address. Just keep in mind the simpler you keep your response, the less identity you will have floating on the internet.

• You may want to set up a free email account (like MSN's Hotmail or YahooMail) to use when you don't want to give away your permanent email account. When setting these up, make sure that you opt-out of all shared information, and again, give as little personal data as possible.

☐ Make sure that the internet sites that you use regularly have your updated address and phone number. You don't want these companies sending statements or other information to an outdated address.

Simplify the Documents in Your Car

☐ Clean all of the identity documents out of your glove compartment. Ideally you would lock these documents up. More practically, place your proof of insurance and car registration in an out of the way place that is easy for you to remember (like an Altoids or Band-Aid canister that fits in the compartment between your seat). Thieves that break into cars generally have to work so quickly that they won't take the extra time to search for documents that aren't in the glove compartment or behind a visor.

☐ For even greater protection, buy a "key lock" combination box like those used by real estate agents and store your sensitive documents in there. Lock the box to the car; the trunk can be a good place. If you get pulled over, explain to the police officer why you keep your information in the trunk *before* you get out of the car.

☐ Keep your repair and oil change receipts locked up in your home filing cabinet. These items are generally only needed when you are selling or have a problem with your car. They do not need to be in the car itself.

Identity theft is more costly when the thief is able to obtain more sophisticated information (e.g., Social Security number, driver's license) that allows him or her to set up completely new accounts:

The average (mean) cost to victims by type of fraud[5]

Fraud committed on existing credit card accounts: **$5,803**

Fraud committed on existing non-credit card accounts: **$9,912**

Fraud committed on new accounts set up in victim's name: **$12,646**

6

The 3rd Mindset— Destroy Private Information

Sometimes the people picking up your garbage don't think of it as trash; they think of it as cash. And sometimes the trash man is really a broker, selling bags of trash to the highest bidder.

Stolen Life #1,336

The Donaldsons had just purchased a new home. They closed on the home on Thursday, removed the For Sale sign on Friday and moved in over the weekend. The following Wednesday was their trash pickup day, and by then, they had plenty of trash.

The garbage was picked up on Wednesday while they were at work. They assumed it had all been taken by the waste and recycling company. They were wrong.

When the Donaldsons removed the For Sale sign, it signaled a local identity theft crime ring (referred to as the Cash Men, instead of the trash men) to pay attention. New owners are a good indication that there will be copies of financial documents in the trash for the next several weeks. They often contain every piece of identity a thief would need—Social Security numbers, birthdates, addresses, phone numbers, bank accounts—all in one convenient pickup. The Cash Men used a trash truck to pick up select bags of information throughout the neighborhood without being suspicious.

The thieves promptly submitted a false change of address that routed the Donaldson's mail to their untraceable P.O. box. By "washing" checks (using finger nail polish remover to change the Pay To field so that the check was made out to the thief), applying for new credit cards with their social security number and taking out a loan, the Cash Men were able to fund a full-scale methamphetamine lab.

The Cash Men knew that because the Donaldsons had just made a major purchase (the house) they probably wouldn't be applying for credit any time soon, which is how most people discover identity theft. And they were right. It was 23 months and tens of thousands of dollars later that the Donaldsons caught on—when the police showed up to arrest them for running a meth lab.

Spies cover their tracks, and so should we. Spies don't mind filtering through trash that pays them well. We must **destroy private information** that we no longer need!

Spy Mindset: Destroy unnecessary information that would cause harm if it were to fall into the hands of the enemy.

Destroy Mindset: Systematically destroy private information that could lead to identity theft if it were to fall into the wrong hands.

Spies cover their tracks by getting rid of the paper trail. When they no longer need a piece of physical information, they throw it in a "burn bag" and it is incinerated. In *Mission: Impossible*, instructions on the next assignment always self-destructed shortly after they were read. However, you don't need to destroy this book!

> *Every act of creation is first an act of destruction.*
>
> — Pablo Picasso

Identity thieves are experts at collecting data that is not properly destroyed. They generally do this by digging through the trash on your curbside or in a company dumpster. In some cases this is even legal as trash is not necessarily your property once it passes through your front door[6]. Spying on your trash is called "dumpster diving."

Thieves also pick up credit card receipts on restaurant tables once the guests have left and before the waiter has picked up the receipt. Sometimes the waiter *is* the thief. Few people realize that credit card masking (covering up all of the numbers except the last four) is only required by law on the customer copy, not the merchant copy. Consequently, the merchant copy often contains your entire credit card number.

To increase your safety, you will need to destroy historical records (old bank statements, tax records, cancelled checks, computer files, etc.) as well as current documents that would otherwise go out in the trash.

There is a simple rule of thumb for what to destroy—anything with a piece of identity on it that will be thrown out with the trash, left in someone else's control or that can't be locked up.

If you are leaving your identity in someone else's hands (the garbage man, the waiter, the sales clerk), your risk of identity theft just escalated. This should trigger alarms and cause you to think twice about leaving your information alone. Use this rule of thumb when you are uncertain of what to destroy. When in doubt, destroy it. There are very few documents that can't be recreated.

Destroying Physical Information (files, documents, credit cards)

A paper shredder is the best means of destroying documents, disks and credit cards. Choosing which documents to keep and which to destroy is a personal choice, and can be difficult. The more you destroy, the less you will need to secure (see next chapter). If you like to keep documents for longer periods, I recommend buying a larger fire-rated filing cabinet or fire-safe and storing these documents securely rather than destroying them.

Place the shredder near to where you open mail or file documents so that you shred what would have normally been thrown away. If you have several locations throughout the house where you deal with these types of documents, collect the papers at each location and shred them once or twice a week before they go into the trash. Make sure that the shredder isn't where small children can get to it. If you don't want to buy a shredder, make sure you tear the documents into small pieces.

Here is a quick list of some of the most vulnerable items that go out in the trash and are good candidates for the shredder:

- ☐ Pre-approved credit card offers
- ☐ Convenience checks from credit card companies
- ☐ Copies of mortgage and loan documents
- ☐ Social Security annual statements
- ☐ Credit card statements
- ☐ Cancelled checks

☐ Bank statements

☐ Credit card receipts

☐ Pay stubs

☐ Utility bills

☐ Phone bills

☐ Cell phone bills

☐ Insurance/Medical statements

☐ Car registration/insurance

☐ Brokerage statements

☐ Copies of tax records or notes

☐ Expired driver's licenses

☐ Expired credit cards

For a further list of items that end up in the trash, refer back to the list on page 33. Also refer to the table in the next chapter, *Secure the Essentials*, for suggestions on which documents to lock up.

The best way to determine what historical financial documents to destroy is by asking your tax accountant or lawyer. There are specific suggestions of what documents to keep in the next chapter, but laws vary by state and you would be well-served to find out from an expert in your area that is familiar with your needs. When this isn't possible, lock the documents up rather than destroying them.

Destroying Digital Information (disks, emails, CDs)

One of the main reasons we destroy old paper files is because they take up space, which can be expensive, especially if you lock them up. With computer files, this is less of an issue. As long as your computer is well protected (see next chapter) and has enough storage space (a large hard drive), you gain little by deleting documents from your computer. If you want to clean files off for the sake of organization, I recommend copying them onto a CD or DVD disk that you protect with passwords or encryption (more complex) or store in your fire-safe (easier).

This is one of the many factors that make a computer such a good way to prevent identity theft. By taking some basic measures, you can lock down your system (and therefore your identity) without going to great lengths. This is discussed further in the next chapter.

There are a couple of exceptions. First, if you are donating or throwing a computer away, you should electronically "shred" the hard drive before you pass it on. This can be done using any number of programs, or performing a low-level format on the hard drive. I recommend leaving this to a computer technician, as it is a very permanent and unrecoverable means of destruction. The data on your computer can be worth thousands; having it professionally deleted or transferred to another computer is a good investment.

Second, if you have a notebook computer, I recommend adding a second level of protection, called encryption. See *Securing the Essentials* for details.

☑ Action Items: Destroy Physical Information

☐ Purchase a paper shredder. Go to your local office supply store or visit *www.thinklikeaspy.com* for our reviews on the best shredders. I recommend the following features:

- Cross-cut confetti shredding. Strip shredders make it too easy to reconstruct documents and often leave account numbers intact along one of the strips.

- 5+ pages of simultaneous feeding capacity. If it takes fewer sheets than this at one time, it is easy to get discouraged with how long it takes to shred documents and you might give up.

- Allows shredding of stapled documents.

- It is convenient to buy one that shreds CD-ROMs and credit cards too, though I'm not sure it is always worth the extra expense. If you only need to destroy a few credit cards and CD-ROMs each year, just use scissors for the credit cards and put the CD-ROMs in a towel to protect your hands and break them. This will save you money and will still get the job done. For added security, throw the cut up or broken sections of credit cards into separate loads of trash to make it impossible to reconstruct.

☐ Start shredding any papers that are going in the trash immediately. Be generous with what you shred—overcompensating won't hurt you (unless you shred something you need).

☐ As you file your latest statements, cancelled checks, tax information, etc., decide if it is time to destroy the outdated copies of these documents. Check with your accountant so that you know what to keep for tax purposes, etc.

☐ Use your new shredder as a reason to clean off the piles of identity on your desk, in your files, and throughout the house. Remember, 50% of identity theft is committed by someone that the victim knows[7]. Identity theft inside of the home is often committed by domestic help, contracted workers, guests and even friends and family. By shredding and locking those sensitive documents, you lessen the temptation for dishonest visitors.

☐ Before selling or donating your computer, make sure you have formatted the hard drive so that your data cannot be reconstructed. If you are throwing away or selling a cell phone, make sure you clean off all of your contacts and information first.

☐ If you own a business, make sure to destroy sensitive documents prior to discarding them to decrease your legal liability.

Effective June 1, 2005, businesses are required to destroy all consumer information before discarding it in the trash. The Fair & Accurate Credit Transaction Act (FACTA) Disposal Rule states that "any person who maintains or otherwise possesses consumer information for a business purpose" **must properly destroy the information prior**

to disposal. FACTA further states that every person and/or business must take "reasonable measures" to protect against unauthorized access to the use of the information in connection with its disposal.

☐ When you are in a restaurant or retail store, scratch out all but the last four digits on the merchant copy of your credit card receipt. They have already processed the number electronically and should not be storing a paper copy of your number and expiration date. Tear up your copy if you don't need it for your records. Tear up any carbon paper if they are using manual swipe receipts.

7

The 4th Mindset—
Secure the Essentials

Unfortunately, spies aren't always strangers. The best physical security (locks, etc.) against intruders does nothing to stop identity thieves. In fact, it probably helps them, because the owner feels so secure from the outside that he or she disregards threats from the inside.

Stolen Life #1,477

Carmen's family was robbed when she was eleven. She will never forget how sick it made her feel that someone had been in her home, prowling around. That is why Carmen, now 36 and with a house larger than most people's dreams, takes particular pride in and spent a fortune on security. Carmen grew up "thinking like a thief," and takes great precautions to protect her home from the outside in.

She lives in a gated community with a security service that monitors the homes 24 hours a day. She also has a $20,000 motion-sensitive burglar alarm and video surveillance system, and two German Shepherds. All of her doors use double-deadbolts that are connected to a thumbprint scanner. When someone wants to enter the house, they press their thumb against a pad just outside any of the doorways. Four people have access by thumbprint—her mother, sister, cleaning lady and best friend.

She describes her home as a "safe house." She shreds every piece of paper that leaves the house, uses encryption technology on her computer, internet connection and wireless network, and only mails documents directly from the post office. Her wallet contains one credit card, one driver's license, a picture of her nephew and no checks. The documents in her car are locked up.

Her identity was stolen completely without her knowledge. Two years later, it was given to the police during an arrest for a crime that she had nothing to do with. The woman (who was not even the identity thief, but someone who had purchased a "new" identity on the internet) held up a pharmacy at gunpoint and was caught because of a flat tire.

Carmen's weakness was the way she stored private documents, or rather, the way she didn't store them. She left tax documents on her desk for weeks without filing them securely.

And the thief? A painter who had asked to use the upstairs bathroom since they were painting the downstairs bathroom. The police think that the painter actually used the small photocopier in her home office to make copies of several documents. None of her papers were ever identified as missing, which is why she never suspected foul play. The painter was later caught stealing documents on another job and confessed to the police about stealing Carmen's information. Carmen is part of the 50% of identity theft victims each year who know their thief.

We must lock up our vital documents as if they were cash, because to an identity thief, they are. Secure the Essentials!

 Spy Mindset: Lock up or conceal anything that would cause harm if it fell into the hands of the enemy.

Secure Mindset: Systematically lock up private information that can lead to identity theft if it falls into the wrong hands.

Spies live a mindset of secrecy. As we learned in the last two chapters, they keep only what they need and destroy any information that has no further use. But their secrecy goes even further. They operate out of **safe houses**, which are information-tight despite being in the middle of enemy territory. Within the safe house, they set up a hacker-proof **command center**, which uses technology to safely store, access, analyze and communicate information via computer. They also use dead-drops as a secure way to send sensitive mail that cannot be communicated electronically.

We will deal with each of these techniques in individual sections.

Family members and relatives are more likely to commit [types of fraud that] have greater total cost, greater out-of-pocket cost and require more time to resolve than frauds committed by other groups of criminals.

— *2005 Identity Fraud Survey Report,* Javelin Strategy & Research

A quick note on the title of this chapter, *Secure the Essentials*. We secure the essentials because everything else was either simplified or destroyed in the two previous chapters. The only identity documents remaining are the essentials. See the table further on in this chapter for examples of what are essential or vital documents.

Creating a Safe House

A safe house is not just a physical location; it is also a way of thinking. A safe house should prompt you to think about who has access into the house (and your information) and what data goes out of the house (access in/data out). Let me explain. Imagine that a safe house is a centralized repository of every piece of intelligence that a spy has collected, or is protecting. It contains dossiers (vital documents) on his targets and informants, information about his true identity and aliases, links to his employer and maybe even other spies that are a part of his network. Because of the value of this information, there are controls on who has access into the house (**access in**), and on what data is allowed out of the house (**data out**). Creating a safe house by controlling access in and data out is a mindset of its own.

These are the same controls that must be implemented in your home. Simply put, anytime a piece of data goes out of the house (via trash, telephone, mail, email, wireless network, human carrier, etc.) or someone is allowed (or illegally gains access) into the house (friends, family, guests, contract laborers, domestic help, thieves), you should have safeguards in place to protect your essential identity documents.

Essential Identity Documents and How to Secure Them

The following chart lists some of your essential identity documents (vital documents), where you should store them, and where to store duplicate copies. Please verify length of storage time with your lawyer, accountant or tax advisor, as these can vary.

TYPE OF STORAGE	DOCUMENT(S)	KEEP A COPY?	WHERE TO STORE DUPLICATE
BANK SAFE DEPOSIT BOX	Birth certificates; death certificates; marriage license; adoption, citizenship, divorce papers	Yes	Home Fire-safe
	Inventory and photos of household property	Yes	Home Fire-safe
	Property deeds, titles, bills of sale, car title, mortgage documents	Yes	Home Fire-safe
	List of location of important papers	Yes	Home Fire-safe, a secure off-site location (friend or relative's fire-safe, attorney's office, etc.)
	Insurance policies	Yes	Home Fire-safe

The documents below need to be protected against fire, flood and theft.

TYPE OF STORAGE	DOCUMENT(S)	KEEP A COPY?	WHERE TO STORE DUPLICATE
FIRE-SAFE or FIRE-RATED, LOCKING FILING CABINET	Tax returns; supporting documents for past 7 years; Social Security cards	No	—
	Passport	Yes	Home Fire-safe. Also, carry a copy of your passport in a different location from the original when you travel.
	Bank-account information	Yes	Secure off-site location
	List of Passwords, PIN #s, Account #s	No	—
	List of all assets, including brokerage and mutual-fund accounts, stocks, bonds, bank accounts, real property, and employee-benefit accounts	Yes	Secure off-site location
	Backup copies of computer documents (CD-R, DVD-R, Tape Backup, Disk)	Yes	Secure off-site location
	Lease agreements; loan documents; rental agreements; vehicle purchase agreements	No	—

The documents below need to be protected against theft.

TYPE OF STORAGE	DOCUMENT(S)	KEEP A COPY?	WHERE TO STORE DUPLICATE
LOCKING FILING CABINET or SECURE COMPUTER	Bank statements	No	—
	Cancelled checks	No	—
	Investment, securities, mutual fund statements	No	—
	Credit card statements	No	—
	Monthly mortgage statements	No	—
	Phone, utilities, cable, cellular statements	No	—
WALLET	Driver's license or other photo I.D.	Yes	Home Fire-safe
	Auto insurance card	Yes	Secured in Car
	Emergency contacts statements	Yes	Home Fire-safe
	Blood type, list of allergies, medications	Yes	Home Fire-safe
	Credit Cards & Other Cards	Yes	Home Fire-safe

☑ Action Items: Secure Your Vital Physical Documents

☐ Buy a fire-safe or fire-rated filing cabinet for your home. This is where you will store your essential identity documents. Go to your local office supply store or visit *www.thinklikeaspy.com* for our reviews on the latest and greatest fire-safes and fire-rated filing cabinets. Save money by purchasing a filing cabinet that is also fire-rated and eliminates the need for a fire-safe and a locking filing cabinet. Your safe or cabinet should meet these minimum requirements:

- Able to withstand 1500° F for 30 minutes

- Lockable by key or combination

- Heavy enough to discourage theft or be secured to the ground

- Preferably waterproof (in case of fire, your house will get wet)
- It is nice to buy stackable units so that your safe storage can expand as your documents expand.

☐ Secure your essential identity documents according to the chart above. Take the following steps:

   ☐ Collect all of the documents that you need to put in a bank safe deposit box (banks charge about $50 per year for a document-sized drawer).

   ☐ Photocopy each of these documents and place the copy in your fire-safe or fire-rated cabinet. For easy reference, keep a log of every document that lives in your bank deposit box (especially for your spouse, who might not be as familiar with the contents).

   ☐ Put the documents in the bank's safety deposit box and put one key in your fire-safe and another in a completely different location (e.g., work). Make sure that your spouse is also able to get into the safety deposit box, as they are generally sealed upon death if there are no surviving co-signers.

These documents are the most important documents in your life and should be kept indefinitely.

☐ Collect and file the remainder of the documents that belong in a fire-safe. Use one hanging file folder per year, with manila folders by subject (bank, brokerage, home, etc.) to store the documents. I suggest keeping seven years of records because it is easy to remember and is an ample amount of time to store most any document. I use a slightly larger fire-rated filing cabinet so that I didn't have to purchase both a fire-safe and a locking filing cabinet.

☐ Collect and file the remainder of the documents in a locking filing cabinet. Shred any statements that have outlived their lifespan each time you file the latest documents (accumulation). Within months you will have a simplified filing cabinet.

☐ Clean up your desk, files and mail area. Use safety as a mandatory reason to clean sensitive papers off of your desk, out of drawers, etc., and centralize them in one secure location.

☐ If you own a business, make sure that your trash dumpsters are locking dumpsters. Give the trash company a key to the padlock. Locking up your trash can greatly decrease your legal liability. As stated in the last chapter:

As of June 1, 2005, businesses were required to destroy all consumer information before discarding it in the trash. The Fair & Accurate Credit Transaction Act (FACTA) Disposal Rule states that "any person who maintains or otherwise possesses consumer information for a business purpose" must properly destroy the information prior to disposal. FACTA further states that every person and/or **business must take "reasonable measures" to protect against unauthorized access** to the use of the information in connection with its disposal.

Setting up a "Command Center"—Securing Your Computer

For many people, a personal computer serves as their primary filing cabinet for financial, legal and personal records. Your computer can either be an asset or a liability in protecting these records. Unprotected, it is a liability because it is open to:

1. Hackers (thieves who break in from your internet or network connection)

2. Spyware (software that broadcasts your personal information to advertisers and thieves without your consent)

3. Viruses (software that damages your data—like Quicken files, Excel spreadsheets, Word documents, tax records, etc.)

4. Old-fashioned thieves (who steal information by sitting at your computer)

Protected, your computer can be one of the safest ways to store sensitive information, pay bills, shop and communicate. The next section will discuss how to use your secure computer to fight identity theft.

First you must ensure that you have a secure computer. Below are several recommendations about securing your computer. Computers are now so vital to our daily lives that I am a firm believer in having a professional computer technician perform these tasks, as they will do a better job than most consumers. Make sure you are using a company that has been around long enough to prove that they are honest (10 years or longer).

The average person doesn't pilot a plane just because they have been a passenger, and they don't install an air conditioner because they have used one before. In the same manner, most people shouldn't assume they fully understand computer security just because they use a computer. You may spend tens or hundreds of dollars to protect your PC, but you will be securing thousands of dollars worth of data and significantly reducing your chances of identity theft in the process. A Social Security number, which links to your retirement benefits and available credit, could be worth $300,000 or more.

I recommend that you make a photocopy of this list, highlight the items that you need to have completed (many computers already have some of these precautions) and give the list to your computer technician. Ask them for an estimate of the work to be completed before you leave your computer. It won't be exact, but it will give you a general idea. The price of computers has gone way down — use the additional funds to protect your PC properly.

☑ Action Items: Secure Your Digital Documents & PC

"Protection software thwarts many online criminal activities."[8]

- ☐ **Anti-Spyware.** Have your computer technician install *and configure* anti-spyware software. Installation is only one step in setting up successful software security. If it is configured (set up) incorrectly, or uses the generic factory defaults, it will not adequately protect you.

Spyware is any program that installs on your computer without your informed consent and most often adversely affects your computer's performance or forwards your personal information to advertisers, competitors or hackers.

Spyware comes in all flavors (adware, malware, etc.)—one of the more malicious forms records every keystroke you make and sends the data to those spying on you. This is one way that credit card numbers, customer records, buying habits, Social Security numbers and other pieces of identity are hijacked from your system. There are common computer symptoms that suggest your system has been infected by spyware: you receive popup ads, your computer or internet connection is running slower, your system or network is crashing more often, the default home page in your browser has recently changed without your consent, your wireless network won't connect, your computer is "acting strangely."

To minimize the impact of spyware:

• Make sure you are having a reputable software package installed. For a review of what anti-spyware software we currently suggest, visit the Reviews section of *www.thinklikeaspy.com*. I recommend that you purchase one of these packages as your primary anti-spyware software because you generally get what you pay for. When you pay for protection, there is usually a reason.

• Make sure the software has the latest security updates and is set to auto-update without user-intervention.

• Make sure the software is set to periodically run a full system scan (weekly).

• In addition, have your technician install one of the free anti-spyware programs as well (like Spy-Bot or Ad-Aware). This gives you an extra layer of protection.

☐ **Anti-Virus.** If you don't already have an anti-virus package (Norton, McAfee) installed and configured, have your computer technician do this as well.

• Make sure you are having a reputable software package installed. We review the best up-to-date packages on our website.

• Make sure it has the latest security updates and is set to auto-update without user-intervention.

• Make sure it is set to run a full system scan periodically (late at night, when you aren't using the computer).

☐ **Windows Updates.** Have your technician configure Windows for automatic security updates. Make sure that you have the latest service packs and updates for your operating system and office software. Failing to keep Windows up to date is like leaving the doors to the castle wide open.

☐ **Firewall.** A firewall is a device that regulates who (from the internet) has access into your data. It can also be used to regulate what data can leave your computer through the internet. If you connect to the internet, and especially if you have high-speed internet access (DSL, cable modem, T1), it is essential to have a firewall installed and configured. This keeps hackers from getting into your system to steal information.

Software firewalls tend to do a better job at keeping unnecessary information from leaving your computer, but they require more processing power (which means they slow your computer down) and can be a bit annoying (you are frequently asked if you want data to leave your computer over the internet).

Hardware firewalls are what most businesses use because you don't sacrifice the performance of individual computers. They can be used to block out specific websites, instant messaging and file downloads. Your computer technician should be able to make a recommendation based on your specific needs and style. We review several packages on our website.

☐ **Wireless Network.** Have your wireless network encrypted so that your data isn't floating in the airwaves for any hacker to intercept. I recommend having your technician setup WEP as well as MAC addressing. This ensures that only your specific computers can get on the wireless network.

☐ **Pop-Up Blocker.** Windows now comes standard with a Pop-Up Blocker. Have your technician turn this on as it reduces the chances that you will accidentally download spyware and viruses onto your system. If you continue to get pop-ups on your computer, make sure to never click on any buttons on the screen (including the "NO" or "Decline" buttons), which will also download spyware onto your system. Instead, click on the Windows "X" at the top right corner of your browser to close the window. Pop-ups that show up even though you have a pop-up blocker are a sure sign that your computer is infected with spyware.

☐ **Phishing Scams.** Learn to understand and recognize phishing scams. Briefly, a phishing scam is an email disguised to look like it is from a familiar source such as your financial institution (bank or brokerage), eBay, PayPal or a host of other financial and ecommerce companies. The email asks you to login to the website by clicking on a link within the email. This link takes you to a website that looks exactly like that of the legitimate financial institution and asks you to input personal information (your identity). This information is used by the phishing thief to access your real account. One such PayPal phishing email I received recently read:

Dear Paypal valued member, It has come to our attention that your account information needs to be updated due to inactive members, frauds and spoof reports. If you could please take 5 to 10 minutes out of your online experience and renew your records you will not run into any future problems. However, failure to update your records will result in account suspension Please follow the link below and login to your account and renew your account information...

The email appeared just as printed above and used actual PayPal logos and colors. It also included all of the typos (PayPal spelled wrong, lack of proper punctuation, etc). Please read Chapter 8, *Observe & Evaluate,* for better tools on not falling victim to phishing schemes. To avoid phishing scams, categorically refuse to enter any information on a website if you navigated there through an email. Instead, type the site into your web-browser and go to your account from there. Very few financial sites have you change information directly through an email.

Visit *www.antiphishing.org* for a better explanation of phishing, and to see real-life examples.

☐ **Backup.** One of the most overlooked forms of security is making a backup copy of your data. If your computer is damaged in a fire or has a hard drive failure, the only way to get the data back is in the form of a backup copy. There are many forms of backup, but I recommend DVD burners, which will backup 8GB of data on disks that cost less than a dollar each. The initial drive should be less than $100. Make a backup of your data (e.g., your My Documents Folder) every week, or anytime you save a highly important document. Store the DVDs in your fire-safe.

☐ **Passwords.** Turn on Windows login passwords for each member of your family so that your private data stays private. You will still be able to share information that you want all family members to access. Have your screen saver default to the password screen after 10 minutes so that when you walk away from your computer, it is still protected (this is available from Windows XP forward).

Spies use passwords to protect just about every piece of information that they collect. Because of the importance of passwords, computer or otherwise, let me take a few paragraphs to suggest a better way to make and store passwords, whether it is for your computer, your ATM card or a website like eBay, PayPal, your bank or brokerage.

• First of all, don't use the same password for everything. If someone has access to that password, they will have access to all of your accounts.

• Second, combine letters and numbers to make cracking your password more difficult. I recommend that you avoid punctuation because you generally can't use it on ATM machines, phone key pads, etc.

• Third, make a series of four passwords of different lengths that you use for different accounts (PIN numbers are usually four digits; internet passwords are usually six-to-eight digits minimum). Make up a set of rules that guide how you create your passwords: For example, if you love flowers, your passwords could be:

L1LL13S   DA1S3S   0RCH1DS   SUNF10W3RS

All I's are replaced by 1's, all E's are replaced by 3's and all O's are replaced by 0's. Now all you have to remember are the four flowers and your set of rules. If you need a password that is all numeric, make sure you choose a completely random number (not one based on birthdays, addresses, etc). You will need to memorize this number.

• If you need to store this information in your address book, contact manager or wallet, store it like this: Bank ATM Password: L (you will have to remember your four flowers—make sure they start with different letters).

• If you currently use one single password for everything, or have passwords that are birthdates, children's names, dog's names, phone numbers, or that don't use both letters and numbers, change them now according to your new scheme. Start with your Windows login passwords and website logins and then move to your ATM PIN, debit card, etc.

• Make a log of your passwords (in case a spouse or relative needs to get into your accounts) and store them in your fire-safe.

• Never send full passwords through email. If you must communicate them, do it by phone.

☐ **Protect your Notebook.** If you have a laptop or notebook computer, make sure you take extra precautions to protect your data. Because of their portability, notebook computers have a much higher risk of being lost or stolen. And when this happens, a thief has as long as they need to break through your passwords. This could mean keeping sensitive documents off of your notebook all together, or using an encryption package like PGP that further protects your portable computer.

☐ **Good Surfing Habits.** Never click on pop-up advertisements while surfing. Stay away from danger areas such as adult entertainment. Teach your kids how to close pop-up ads (using the "X" box) as children's websites are notorious for spyware and viruses.

☐ **Secure Shopping.** When you are buying an item over the web, make sure it is with a reputable company. Also, in the bottom right corner of your browser, look for the small symbol of a closed lock, which means that the site you are buying from uses SSL encryption (which is a type of computer security that protects your data as it is transmitted). If the site is not operating on a secure server (i.e., no lock or opened lock), think twice about shopping there. Your credit card will be traveling across the internet unprotected. Either call and make the transaction over the phone or email them to see if they have a secure website where transactions can take place.

☐ **Spouse or Partner.** Don't forget to implement the same safeguards at work and on other computers in your home.

How a Computer Helps to Prevent Identity Theft

Once your computer is secure, it has many advantages over traditional filing systems:

1. It is locked anytime you are not on the computer (thanks to passwords).

2. You can allow different levels of access for different people (thanks to user profiles that are based on usernames and passwords). With a filing cabinet, one key lets everyone into everything.

3. You can store vast quantities of data without taking up physical space. This eliminates the need to destroy physical documents, which saves you time.

4. It can replace one of the most vulnerable avenues of identity theft—mail. By receiving statements and paying bills online, you are less vulnerable to red-flagging (mail theft).

5. When data arrives via email, internet, etc., it is already partially filed, as it already exists on your hard drive. You may choose to save it in a different location, but either way, it is protected. It never exists in an unlocked state, like mail does.

6. You can review online statements more quickly, which means that you catch inconsistencies faster than if you are waiting for the mail. Identity theft victims who monitored their accounts online had an average of $551 stolen and discovered the fraud in an average of 18 days. Those who monitored through paper statements had an average of $4,543 stolen and it took them an average of 114 days to detect the fraud.[9] **Rapid detection is half the battle!**

7. You can add additional layers of protection quite easily if your data is extremely valuable. For about $69, you can buy software that encrypts your hard drive (makes your data a collection of nonsense to anyone who doesn't have the encryption key or password).

8. Note that 68.2% of identity theft is committed using paper rather than electronic methods of obtaining information.[10]

☑ Action Items: Use Your Computer to Prevent Identity Theft

☐ **Replace paper statements that arrive through the mail and sit out on desks** with online statements that are automatically stored in your computer. The Better Business Bureau's first recommendation for the prevention of identity theft is to move to online statements and bill paying.[11] By replacing paper bills, statements and checks with paperless versions (on the internet), you eliminate the risk of having them stolen out of your mailbox (which was also discussed in the tasks section of Chapter 5, *Simplify your Identity*).

• The next time you receive a statement of any kind in the mail, call the customer service number on the statement and ask them to move you to electronic statements. Make sure that they stop your paper statements. Over the course of a month, you should have moved almost every statement from paper to electronic. Don't forget to opt-out of information sharing while you are on the phone with them.

Most electronic statements come in the form of an Adobe Acrobat (or PDF) file. These can be saved directly to your hard drive in a folder named for their specific purpose (e.g., 2005 Schwab Statements—Account 4299).

• When you are online with your first statement, set up auto-alerts (if the company offers them) that alert you to any major activity on the account. For example, with E★Trade you can set up auto alerts that email you when certain transactions occur on your account. This is a great way to monitor your finances on a daily basis without much time investment.

☐ **Stop paying bills through the mail with paper checks.** As you have probably noticed throughout this book, one of the best ways to prevent identity theft is to stop using the mail system for sensitive documents. There are several ways to pay bills without sending a check through the mail.

• **Auto Pay.** Set up auto-pay by credit card. You can generally do this with most major companies (phone bill, utilities, cable TV, insurance, etc.). You can also pay by credit card on a month-by-month basis on most websites. This isn't as convenient, but gives you more control over your charges. I like this option the best as it gives you an easy method to dispute charges (you call the credit card company and freeze the payment until your dispute is settled). In addition, your liability is only $50 if you report fraud in a reasonable time frame.

- **Electronic Funds Transfer.** Since you cannot pay a credit card with a credit card (well, technically you can, but we won't go into that), you will have to pay by other means. You can set up an electronic funds transfer between your bank and the bank of the company you owe money. For example, many insurance agencies don't allow credit card payments, but will automatically deduct your premium each month directly from your bank account. I use this option if the credit card option is not available and if I trust the company who will be withdrawing the funds.

- **Bill Pay.** You can use an electronic bill-payment service, which is offered by most banks, brokerages and many other sources. This is a good third option. Most of the electronic bill-payment services still cut paper checks and send them through the mail. This reduces the risk that an outgoing check will be stolen from your mailbox, but not the risk of it being stolen from the bill-payer's mail, or in transit.

Securing Your Mail

In the modern world of espionage, a majority of communication between a spy and his network happens by computer. Sending documents electronically is very low profile, easy to protect (encrypt) and instant, giving counter-spies (thieves) little time to intercept the data. But there are times when information cannot be sent electronically. This is when spies use a dead-drop, or a secret location where materials can be left by one person and retrieved by another.

This section is doubly important for people who do not have or choose not to use a computer to receive online statements and pay bills. As discussed earlier in the book, it is important that you take prevention steps that fit with your lifestyle. If a computer doesn't fit with the way you wish to receive statements or correspondence, the chances are good that you won't implement those changes. Instead, implement the non-computing version of protecting your mail listed below.

Many people find it entirely unbelievable that mail is stolen so easily.

They think of mail almost like a public service (like the electricity to your home, for example) that rarely falters. Because it is convenient to mail documents, we make excuses and drop them in the box.

Think for a minute about the safety of mailing sensitive documents incorrectly:

> At a recent lecture sponsored by the U.S. Postal Inspection Service (the mail police), the inspector responsible for my region of the country strongly recommended that people should not leave incoming or outgoing mail in unlocked mailboxes like the ones in front of their homes.
>
> He also recommended that we not put outgoing mail in the blue USPS drop boxes, even in front of the post office. He said that these boxes are regularly stolen, are too often "dummy boxes" that don't belong to the mail service or have had the bottoms cut out and replaced by cardboard. The contents are picked up after dark by midnight mailmen (identity thieves). It's believed that most of these crimes are being committed by methamphetamine drug rings that steal identities to fund their illegal drug activities.
>
> Finally, 8% of all known identity theft is committed by mail fraud. But mail fraud is very difficult to catch, which means that the numbers are probably significantly higher. Just by changing this one habit (mailing documents unsafely) you can reduce your chances of identity theft by at least 8%.

☑ Action Items: Secure Your Mail Against Theft

☐ **Stop using the mail to send and receive identity documents.** This is the best solution (as described above in the computer section) but not always possible. Therefore, here are alternative suggestions:

☐ **Lock Box.** Install a locking mailbox that can be accessed only by you. These generally have a mail slot that allows the postal service to put mail into the box. Many newer neighborhoods already have some form of locking mailboxes.

☐ **P.O. Box.** If a locking mailbox is not possible, get a P.O. box at your local post office and have sensitive documents sent there. It is a little bit more work, but gives you much more privacy.

☐ **In Person.** When mailing sensitive documents, walk them into the post office and hand them to a postal worker. If it is after hours, drop the mail through an internal slot in the building. If there is no internal mailing slot, mail it the following day. This cuts out the most vulnerable stages of mailing.

☐ **UPS/FedEx.** Have identity documents sent by UPS or FedEx and make sure that you require a signature for delivery. This makes the information harder to steal and you can track its location at anytime, which will alert you if the document isn't delivered in a timely manner or is diverted somewhere else.

☐ **Send Checks to the Bank.** Have sensitive documents (like new checks or credit cards) sent to your bank rather than to your home address. Pick them up there.

☐ **Watch for Cards.** When new credit cards are coming through the mail, watch for them and call the credit card company if they don't arrive in 7 to 10 days.

☐ **Quick Retrieval.** If you are unable to install a locking mailbox and don't have access to P.O. boxes, retrieve any mail within an hour or two of delivery. This lowers the exposure time of your mail.

☐ **Review Chapter 5,** *Simplify Your Identity* for tips on cutting down the amount of mail that arrives at your home.

"The single most effective approach to protect
against both external and domestic identity theft is
to turn off all paper bills and statements."

— *The 2005 Identity Fraud Survey Report,*
Javelin Strategy & Research

8

The 5th Mindset—
Observe & Evaluate

The enemy does its homework. Whether they are thieves, spies or terrorists, they observe their targets, evaluate the situation according to certain criteria and prepare themselves based on that knowledge. We are foolish if we don't prepare ourselves against them with just as much diligence.

Stolen Life #2,041

Just weeks before the tragic 9/11 attacks, the actor James Woods was flying cross-country to Los Angeles. On the flight, he noticed four well-dressed Middle Eastern men traveling together.

In an interview with Seymour Hersh of The New Yorker, *in June of 2002, Woods commented "I watch people like a moviemaker…I thought these guys were either terrorists or F.B.I. guys." Woods, viewing the situation through the lens of a moviemaker, observed what many of us wouldn't have:*

"These guys were in synch—dressed alike. They didn't have a drink and were not talking to the stewardess. None of them had a carry on or a newspaper. Nothing. Imagine you're at a live-music event at a small night club and you're standing behind the singer. Everybody is clapping, going along, enjoying the show—and there's four guys paying no attention. What are they doing here?"

Woods was suspicious that the four men were "casing" the plane, so he alerted the flight attendant. According to Mr. Hersh's story, when Woods was later shown photographs of the 9/11 hijackers, he thought he recognized two of them—Hamza Alghamdi, who flew on United Flight 175, which destroyed the south tower of the World Trade Center, and Khalid Almihdhar, who was on American Airlines Flight 77, which struck the Pentagon.

Woods told Hersh that he recognized one of the men because of his "pointy hair" and the other because he resembled one of the characters in the movie version of spy novelist John le Carre's "The Little Drummer Girl."

James Woods's heightened sense of observation triggered his instinct of danger. He had noticed other passengers acting out of character (no luggage or reading materials, dressed identically and isolated from the flight attendants) and took action. If his hunch had been taken seriously, the outcome of 9/11 might have been different.

Spy Mindset: Spies are aware of virtually everything happening around them. They are able to make quick decisions because they are prepared at all times for the enemy.

Observe & Evaluate Mindset: We must closely observe virtually everything that involves our vital information or identity in order to protect it.

The 5th Mindset, *Observe and Evaluate*, is actually a combination of two behaviors that cannot be easily separated, as they occur in the same breath. We observe a situation and immediately make a judgment on what is happening. For example, we see someone lurking in the shadows of a doorway in the next block (observe) and make the decision (evaluate) to cross the street away from potential danger.

Spies are masters at this. Their skills include:

- Monitoring any changes in their environment (which can signal trouble)

- Ignoring their assumptions about a situation (things aren't always as they appear)

- Watching their backs in the field (you never know who the enemy is)

- Maintaining a healthy skepticism about sharing information

- Making snap judgments about issues of risk and safety

When they are out in the field (spying), they are hyper-aware of their surroundings. We must use these same skills to protect our identity. But we are at a distinct disadvantage.

The Problem—A World of Distracted Zombies

To be honest, many of us are walking around in a fog of distraction. We talk on our cell phones between bites of bagel as we steer the car to our next destination and have the nerve to ask our kids to pipe down so that we can think. Yeah, right. To the outside observer, someone who actually stops and watches, we must look like zombies. To those readers who are not constantly distracted, I congratulate and envy you.

The American poet, Theodore Roethke, said, "A mind too active is no mind at all."

Identity thieves take advantage of our distracted minds. We must slow down and learn to observe our surroundings and evaluate what we see, especially when our identity is "in play."

Some people are naturally more observant. They notice when the tire on their car is low without consciously thinking about it. They look to see who is behind them at the ATM machine as a matter of habit. The rest of us need help with our powers of observation. Because we are in a hurry or have other things on our mind, we act without thinking things through.

Observation is a difficult and intangible skill to teach (and learn), because it is really nothing more than asking someone to see what is already in front of them. For example, look at the diagram below and count the number of squares:

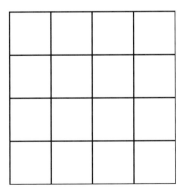

Before we get to the answer, did you come up with your answer in five seconds or less? I have found in my speeches that audiences tend to be more concerned with the speed of their answer than with accuracy. **We have been pre-conditioned to answer rapidly.** If your answer was fewer than 17, take more time with the puzzle after reading through the following **heightened observation** process:

The author just suggested that many people are distracted. Could that be me? He is attempting to teach me about the power of observation and is giving me a test to see if my answer is pre-conditioned. Don't answer immediately; there is something that I am probably missing here. What haven't I thought of? Could there be a different number of squares than the obvious answer?

The squares can be counted in groups of one (for a total of sixteen squares), as well as being combined into squares made up of four smaller squares (nine combinations), nine smaller squares (four combinations) and sixteen smaller squares (one combination). The correct answer is thirty. If you didn't get it right, don't feel bad, it took me five tries and several reams of paper. My power of observation sometimes doesn't reach beyond my eyelashes. (If you counted all thirty on the first try, you should look into espionage as a full-time profession.)

The point of this exercise has little to do with getting the correct answer. It is to demonstrate that our assumptions (and pre-conditioning) are very powerful, and can get in the way of effective observation. In this example, we have been pre-conditioned to answer the

Get out now. Not just outside, but beyond the trap of the pro-grammed electronic age so gently closing around so many people at the end of our century. Go out-side, move deliberately, then relax, slow down, look around. Do not jog. Do not run. Forget about blood pressure and arthri-tis, cardiovascular rejuvenation and weight reduction. Instead, pay attention to everything that abuts the rural road, the city street, the suburban boulevard. Walk. Stroll. Saunter. Ride a bike, and coast along a lot. Explore.

—John Stilgoe, *Outside Lies Magic*

puzzle quickly rather than to *puzzle* on it. Is it because we believe that the faster we answer, the smarter we appear? Is it our competitive nature, or a desire to impress others?

Regardless of the source of pre-conditioning, pointing it out tends to eliminate the conditioning. If I were to give you a second puzzle, you would look at it more closely. Voíla, your powers of observation have been sharpened.

To increase our power of observation in regard to our identity, we must first know what to look for, what pre-conditions exist, and how to respond.

The Solution: Knowing How to Observe

Ideally, over time, we will learn to set aside our distractions throughout the day to observe and enjoy life on a higher level as it is happening. More practically, we need to have a mechanism, as we started to discuss in Chapter 3, which triggers this heightened sense of observation when our identity is at risk. We need to relearn how to observe with a keener eye.

The Trigger, Reaction & Response Technique

The Trigger—Any Contact with Your Identity!

Outside access to your *identity in any form* is the trigger. Anytime someone requests or has access to any of the names, numbers or attributes that make up your identity, or to the paper, plastic, digital or human data where your identity lives, the trigger should trip and sound an alarm in your head.

Here are some situations that should serve as **triggers**:

- When you are pulling out your **wallet, purse, checkbook** or **credit card**

- When you are putting a document into the **trash** or **filing cabinet**

- When you are sending a piece of **mail**

- When you are clicking on a link in an **email**

- When you are entering data into a **website**
- When you are using an **ATM** machine or **PIN** pad
- When you receive a **call** requesting information
- When you notice sensitive documents lying on your **desk** at home or work
- When you are opening an **account**
- When anyone **requests** your personal information
- When you are voluntarily **sharing** any piece of your identity
- When you are involved in any sort of **money** or **credit** transaction
- When you are answering a **survey** or entering a **contest**
- Anytime you are filling out **forms** that request a piece of your identity

The Reaction—Actually Think the Word *"SPY!"*

Your immediate reaction to the trigger, the alarm that sounds in your mind loud and clear, should be the word *SPY!* Until proven innocent (and innocence will be the case 99% of the time), you should regard this person or situation as identity creep.

The Pre-conditions that Cloud Our Reactions

Like Pavlov's dogs (who followed directions in exchange for doggy biscuits), we have been pre-conditioned to give our private information away in exchange for short-term rewards.

We have been desensitized to the value of our data. We give it away to win contests, to download music, to gain access to websites, to receive discounts, to avoid confrontation, to gain convenience, to earn points…and as we add to our pile of doggy biscuits, we weaken the strength of our privacy. There are many pre-conditions that thieves exploit to steal our identities. Some of the most common include:

- Someone wants to give you a **gift** in exchange for your information. The pre-condition operating here is that we undervalue our personal data and consequently exchange it for impulse-based rewards that are of a lesser value (but satisfy a short-term desire).

To combat this, recognize the monetary value of your information. The individual pieces of your identity are as valuable as the assets connected to them. Your Social Security number can be attached to your credit rating, your home, your retirement benefits, unemployment, etc. As my father taught me at a young age, at least in the business world, *there is no such thing as a free lunch*. If you are getting something, you are giving something.

For example, when someone offers you a 10% discount on your purchase if you sign up for their credit card, calculate how much you will be saving in exchange for access to your credit history, address, telephone, etc. This may be a legitimate company, but the alarm is sounding to protect you from identity creep, not immediate identity theft. If you are purchasing $200 worth of clothing, ask yourself if the $20 discount is worth one more company having access to your information—or many companies if the information is sold.

- Someone **threatens** to take away your privileges or rights of access. They might threaten to close, suspend or cancel your account if you don't comply with their request. This preys upon several pre-conditions: our dislike of confrontation, our hesitation to tell someone "no," and our fear of being disliked.

To be blunt, get over it. In instances of identity creep, look at confrontation, answering "no" and being disliked as the price of privacy. There are very few privileges that are worth having your identity stolen.

For example, when an email threatens to close or suspend your account if you don't comply with their request for information, red flags should appear and you should suspect a scam. No profit-driven company in their right mind wants to lose your business, especially if you are a good customer. If you feel that the email could be legitimate, follow up with the company by phone, or visit your account on their website.

- Someone asserts that what he or she is doing is for the "sake of **security**." The pre-condition here is that the thief is removing any pre-condition of skepticism that we might have by "naming the evil." We say to ourselves, *If someone is acting on behalf of security, they couldn't possibly be a fraud. They wouldn't just bring it up!* Wrong. They might be playing the role of the "double agent." If someone involved with your identity uses the word security, fraud, safety, help or any other term that is meant to make you feel like they are doing you a great service, grow suspicious. They are probably either committing the fraud they are promising to protect you against, or selling you something.

  For example, when a computer technician calls your office and starts requesting information about your computers for the sake of security or to help you avoid fraud, you should turn up your observation.

More examples of pre-conditions are included in the next chapter.

The Response, Part 1—Stop, Look and Listen

When an outsider has access to your identity (Identity Creep), which activates the trigger (*SPY!*), your first response should be to heighten your level of Observation. View the situation as a child would—with curious eyes. You can even borrow what we teach our children to be more aware in dangerous situations—Stop, Look and Listen:

Stop what you are doing. Reject the pressure to multitask and be more efficient. Don't talk on your cell phone or think about what you need to do next. Reject the assumption that faster is better. Slow down and be present only to what is happening right around you. Don't answer questions, hand over forms or type a response until you are comfortable with the situation.

Look at the world around you. Bring out your spy lens and be more critical. Is someone peering over your shoulder at the ATM or while you are entering a password into the computer? Does the ATM machine look like it usually does? Is someone hanging around your mailbox or looking at your purse? Is the document on your desk sensitive? The best way to remind yourself to look is to stand there with nothing else to do.

Listen to your instincts. Ask yourself if your identity is safe. Is there a change in the environment that makes you uneasy or uncertain? What is your gut saying? Would a spy give away this information? Is the benefit you are receiving worth the data you are sharing? Do you feel as if you shouldn't ask questions (which generally means you should)? Be a healthy skeptic (i.e., not paranoid, but aware) of anyone who is requesting your identity. Act on your instincts, as James Woods did in the example at the start of the chapter.

The Response, Part 2—A Spy C.A.N. Evaluate the Situation

Now that you have accurately observed your surroundings, evaluate the information gathered by testing it against a set of standards. An easy way to remember the standards is with the phrase **A Spy C.A.N. Evaluate**. The acronym C.A.N. prompts you to analyze the situation for aspects of Control, Access and Necessity.

<u>Control</u>

The first question you should ask yourself is:

Who is in control of this situation?

Are you the one that started the process, or was it initiated by someone else (potentially an identity creep)? Most cases of identity theft happen when an outsider initiates contact with you, not vice versa. They call you on the phone, send you an email, visit you at home or work, or approach you in the mall.

When your Trigger has been activated, I recommend that you use the saying *Initiate or Terminate* to govern how you act. If you didn't start the interaction, you are not in control of the interaction. Your first step should be to take back control by terminating the exchange. You can do this by calling the person back (on a verified number), visiting the person's website directly (rather than clicking on an email link), verifying his or her credentials, etc. These are discussed at length in Chapter 9, *Interrogate the Enemy*.

Access

Then ask yourself:

What information am I allowing them to access?

Your response will be influenced by how sensitive the data is that you are giving away. You will interrogate someone requesting your Social Security number far more than someone asking for your first name. Don't forget that spies are experts at accumulating small pieces of information over time. They may ask you for one piece of identity here, another there. Be aware of how much access you give to any one source over time.

You also should ask yourself:

Who will have access to the information?

When you enter a contest by giving your name, address and yearly income, literally hundreds of people will see that information. Your data is collected, combined with credit records (purchased elsewhere) and aggregated into a profile of who you are, what you are worth, and what products and services you might buy. Your information is not going to one person on the other end of the line, it is being sold to anyone who wants to know more about you.

When you mail a check, anyone who wants to steal your mail has access to your bank account numbers, name, address and signature. When you leave a credit card receipt on the table after you have left the restaurant, you are leaving your credit card number, your name and your signature. Restaurants that deliver food will also have your full address and phone number in their database. And their employees have access to that information.

Necessity

Finally, ask yourself:

Is it necessary to expose my identity in this way?

This is nothing more than a risk/reward analysis. Am I receiving something of equal or greater value for what I am giving? Remember, we have been pre-conditioned to think of our identity as less valuable than the assets to which it is connected.

Can you still receive the long-term benefit without giving the information? Could you pay the bill without sending a check through the mail? Will you still have a warranty on your refrigerator if you don't fill out the "Warranty Survey Card"?

In many cases, you will be able to receive the benefits without giving the information. In other cases, you will decide that you would rather have privacy than the short-term benefit. The key is to ask yourself if it is really worth the cost of identity creep.

✔️ Action Items: Practice Observation & Evaluation

The best way to learn to observe and evaluate situations more closely is to walk though several scenarios and attach the concepts as we go. With enough practice, this mindset should become a habit that doesn't take conscious thought. We will apply the skills of Trigger (Identity), Reaction (*SPY!*), 1st Response (Stop, Look & Listen) and 2nd Response (C.A.N.) and make a decision about how you would go forward.

At first, this approach seems to be a bit paranoid. It appears that way because we are using it as an educational tool to develop good habits. When you learned math, you did it by understanding each step in the process independently, not by having someone say, "Do math." Once you have done it a few times, the process will become second nature and you won't have to think through or name the individual steps. In the meantime, it needs to be a conscious, learning effort. When you are comfortable with your handling of the scenario, check it off the list:

☐ **Protecting Your Identity at an ATM.** You approach an ATM (trigger) and pull out your wallet (trigger). You remove your debit card (trigger). Thanks to the three triggers, you can't help but smile to yourself as you think *SPY!* (reaction), which is a humorous but helpful warning to put your guard up.

Your level of observation increases and you begin to evaluate the situation (response). You take a few seconds (stop) and look to see if anyone is watching over your shoulder to steal your PIN number (look). You look at the ATM machine to make sure that there aren't any devices (skimmers or hidden cameras) that aren't normally there (look). You look for anything out of place or any people that shouldn't be there and your instincts say that you are safe (listen).

You are the one who approached the ATM to make a withdrawal, meaning that you have initiated the situation and are reasonably in control (control). You need the money (necessity) and don't have time to go inside to the bank, so you make the withdrawal.

☐ **Protecting Your Credit Card at a Restaurant.** You are in a restaurant having dinner with friends and are about to pay the check with a credit card (trigger). The waiter is going to take your credit card to another part of the restaurant to run the charges and will therefore be alone with your identity. Since you are aware that this is one of the most popular ways for thieves to steal your identity (by skimming your information on a pocket scanner), you think SPY! (reaction).

You are uncertain about how to respond, because you feel like you will look foolish to your friends if you make a big deal out of letting the credit card disappear. You have several options:

• **Simplify Your Identity—Pay with Cash.** Ask yourself if you have to pay with a credit card (necessity). This old-fashioned way of paying has absolutely zero identity creep. Pay with cash when you don't want to let your card out of your sight or don't want to share information that will ultimately be stored in a database and sold to other businesses (companies buy your credit card histories so that they can market other services to you. They know that if you like to eat at certain restaurants, you will also probably buy their product).

• **Observe Your Card.** If the waiter stays in view, watch to make sure your card is safe. Take comfort in looking foolish from the fact that you will be safe.

• **Pay at the Counter.** Take your credit card up to the cashier and pay there. That way, your card will never be out of your sight (control).

• **Do Nothing and Rely on *Plan B.*** Despite all of our training, this is probably what most of us will still do—let the card disappear with the waiter. Breaking the credit card habit seems to be particularly difficult, which means that we need another way to protect our identity when our information is out of our control. We do this by having a backup plan—a way to protect ourselves when everything else fails. By monitoring our credit card statement, we will catch any fraudulent charges. Chapter 10, *Plan B*, gives us that backup plan in full detail.

☐ **Protecting Your Identity from Phishing Email Scams.** You receive an email from your bank (trigger) saying that your account information (trigger) is out of date and you need to click on the link (trigger) to make updates. Your account will be cancelled if you don't comply (trigger). All of these contacts with your identity trigger you to think SPY!

Your instincts say that it is a legitimate request because it uses the bank's logo and the link you are clicking has the website address of the bank on it. Regardless, you evaluate the request. You were not the one to initiate the request and are therefore not in control of the situation (control).

You have no idea of who will have access to this information, whether it is at the bank or otherwise (access). You don't know what information you will be giving access to, as you haven't clicked on the link to see. From your accumulated knowledge, you guess that it will be fairly sensitive information, including account numbers and passwords.

You ask yourself if it is really necessary to share the information in this way (necessity). Because you have been educated about phishing, you decide that there are other ways to verify that your account is out of date. You close your email and log into your bank account to look for alerts from the bank that your information is incorrect. There are none, so you visit the My Account page and see that everything is up to date. Finally, you call the bank to ask them (interrogate) what the email was all about. They tell you that it is a phishing scam and that you should ignore further requests.

9

The 6th Mindset—
Interrogate the Enemy

Spies often get information by simply asking. Unfortunately, it is that simple.

Stolen Life #2,771

Steve's medical office received a call from Dr. Thompson, a physician from another state. Dr. Thompson explained that he was currently researching software packages for his office and, knowing that Steve's office was well run, wanted to find out what Steve's office used and how they liked it.

Figuring that the questions were harmless, Steve told him that they used PatientTracker 8.0 and were very happy. Dr. Thompson thanked him, and just before hanging up, asked if Steve would give him the name of the technician they worked with at the software company so that he could ask additional questions. Steve gladly told him that their contact at the software company was Jeremy and gave him the phone number.

Thirty seconds later, "Dr. Thompson" called Steve's office a second time and reached the receptionist. He told her that his name was Phil, that he was from PatientTracker Software, and that he was filling in for Jeremy while he was out sick. After flattering her ("Your boss, Steve, says you run a tight office"), he explained that he needed to make a security update (version 8.1) to their software system. It needed to happen soon because their computer system, as configured now, was at risk.

Because Jeremy was out of the office, Phil explained, he didn't have the username and password to dial in to their server and make the changes. He told her that as soon as the changes were made, she would need to change her password to keep the system safe.

Knowing that PatientTracker was their software system, that Jeremy was their technician, that they were currently using version 8.0 and that she didn't want to be respon-

sible for a security risk, the receptionist had no reason to believe she was being tricked. She gave him the password and full access to thousands of private patient records.

We need to begin asking questions of those who ask for personal information. Interrogate the Enemy!

Spy Mindset: Spies gather most of their sensitive information by asking questions. People are only too willing to share their vast knowledge on private matters.

Interrogate Mindset: When in doubt about the security of our identity, we must ask direct questions. Interrogation is the art of questioning someone thoroughly and assertively to verify facts.

When spies need information, they ask for it. They "**socially engineer**" or con their victims with a variety of tools (as we saw in Steve's scenario on the previous page).

> *No man really becomes a fool until he stops asking questions.*
>
> —Charles P. Steinmetz

- They **impersonate** someone who has access or power (a repairman, IT support, a manager, an executive assistant, an account manager, etc.) (Jeremy's colleague).

- They lower your guard first with **flattery** (Steve's office was well run).

- They **accumulate** important data over several conversations (several phone calls).

- They **rush** you to simulate a "crisis" mode (where people forget to think).

- They use **scare tactics** to put you into crisis mode (your system is at risk).

- They **intimidate** you to convince you to back down.

- They lower your self-esteem by demonstrating superior **authority** (doctor).

- They put you **at ease** by claiming that it is for security purposes or to prevent fraud.

- They **drop names** of colleagues, especially those in authority (your boss Steve..., Jeremy your tech...).

- They gain your **trust** by baiting you with accurate background data (PatientTracker, Version 8.1).

- They provide **diversions** by starting the conversation with small talk and end with a memorable, totally unrelated story (our brain remembers the beginning and end of a conversation, but tends to forget the middle).

Most importantly, **spies exploit our human biases and weaknesses**. They take advantage of our pre-conditioning, our basic assumptions about people, which we started to discuss in the previous chapter.

- Humans are trusting by nature (Steve and receptionist).

- Giving this small piece of information, by itself, can't hurt me (PatientTracker).

- People are generally good (I am).

- Don't question people with authority (doctors).

> *He is educated who knows how to find out what he doesn't know.*
>
> — George Simmel

- Helping people is admirable (assisting a colleague).

- Don't slow down a person who's in a hurry (security threat).

- Sharing information makes me feel important (I'm an expert).

- Confrontation is unhealthy.

- Saying "no" is bad.

- Asking for identification or verification is pushy.

We let these biases stand in the way of common sense. To avoid confrontation, we actually explain away our own doubts without considering the other person's intentions. At times, the other person is an identity thief who banks on our biases.

When any form of information or identity is being requested, we can ask ourselves a series of questions to further *evaluate* if we are being spied on. This self-questioning is an extension of observing and evaluating as covered in the last chapter:

- Who is in control of this situation? Who initiated contact?
- What information will this give them access to? Who will have access?
- Is it necessary for me to give away this information?
- Is someone I don't even know flattering me?
- Are they making me feel more important and knowledgeable than a stranger should?
- Do they ask for crucial information in the middle of small talk?
- Are they in a rush? Are they rushing me? Is there a crisis?
- Is this a matter of security?
- Is there an unreasonable consequence for not acting, like closing an account?
- Do they outwardly assert their authority?
- Do they name drop?
- Do they know small bits of information about me?
- Do they introduce meaningless small talk, especially at the beginning or end of the conversation?

If you answer yes to several of these questions, or instinctually feel uneasy, you should be on the alert for an identity creep. **Reaction: *SPY!***

Let's say a gentleman from the local bank calls you with a request for information. You feel uneasy about the conversation.

Response: Abruptly ask him to hold on. Without hesitating, put him on **hold** for a full minute and don't give him a reason why. If you are at home, stick your phone in the drawer. If he hangs up, it was probably a fraud. When you don't explain why you are putting him on hold, he thinks you have caught on to him. He now has visions of FBI phone-traces dancing through his head. This is called "putting him on ice."

If this is happening in person, you will have to think quickly or stall in another way. Bathroom trips, imaginary incoming cell-phone calls, and the like will give you a bit of stall time. Going straight into interrogation mode is another avenue—*Why do you need my information?*

Response, Part 2: While you are on hold, pull out a copy of the 6 Techniques of Interrogation listed below. The questions go from non-confrontational to confrontational. Don't ask the confrontational questions first, as it alerts the caller to trouble before he has had a chance to incriminate himself. Any legitimate person should make it through each successive step without hanging up.

The 6 Techniques of Interrogation

Do not hesitate to be direct—you are now in interrogation mode—take control of the situation.

1. **Ask Why or How.** Your first response should always be to ask why or how. *And how do you know about our office?* This gives you time to think and evaluate his answer. If he is a fraud, he will be well practiced at answering this question. As you continue to ask more detailed questions, fraudulent stories will begin to deteriorate. *Why do you need that information? Why should I give it to you? How did you get my name?*

2. **Set him up to lie.** Feed him a piece of credible, but false, information to see if he takes the bait. *Oh, you are the one that filled in for Jeremy when he broke his leg, right?... I thought you were going to quit after that whole mess....Can you tell me the date you performed the last software upgrade?* You may need to verify these answers before going on.

3. **Let's talk about me**. Ask him to tell you more about you. *Hey, can you tell me the last time I made a purchase on that credit card; I feel like I haven't used it in ages?... How long has our office used this software?* If he is a spy, he won't know any of the real answers.

4. **Let me call you back.** Tell him that you need to give him a ring back. *I've got to take another call. Where can I give you a call back?* An identity thief will almost never give you a legitimate number (crime rings sometimes have temporary phone numbers). *Can I call you back using the number listed on my credit card, bank statement, phone book, etc.)?* When he says that he doesn't have a direct line, and will have to call you back, move to more confrontational questions, like:

5. **Ask if he's an identity thief.** *Let's assume you are an identity thief (chuckle). How can you prove to me you are not?... How can you prove to me that you are who you say you are?... If I can't call you at the number I always use to call our tech support, how can I trust you?... Why is your area code on my caller ID showing a different location than where you guys are based?* These types of questions tend to throw anyone off, so give the person a minute to recover. In espionage, this is called "requesting their Bonafides"—proof that they are who they say they are. This is how spies keep from giving information to counter-spies. You need to validate the person's information so you are comfortable.

6. **Ask for his supervisor.** Most conversations shouldn't have to go this far to identify a legitimate request, but if they do, move up the ladder. Every type of financial institution that has your personal information has a supervisor that will be able to look in his or her system's notes to see what you have already talked about. See if the supervisor has the same story as he does. Modify the data the first person gave and feed it back to the supervisor. *The other tech said that you are putting version 8.6 on the system—is that correct? Are you Tony, our regular technician's boss?*

Don't be afraid to ASK MORE QUESTIONS. Fraudulent stories tend to crumble about three or four questions deep. Finally, don't be afraid to

SAY NO! Tell them that you need to check on some things and will get back to them. Anyone who can't give you time to research is either a fraud or too high-strung to be dealing with.

✓ Action Items: Practice Interrogating the Enemy

In the situations below, assume that you have already observed and evaluated the situation, but haven't been able to determine if you are at risk. Possibly your instinct is prompting you to inquire further. Interrogation is a perfect tool for situations that aren't black and white.

☐ You are buying a new car and paying cash. The sales rep, Susan, asks for your Social Security number. What questions would you ask?

> *Why do you need my Social Security number if I am not paying with credit?*
>
> *Can I still get the car without giving the number?*
>
> *Are you prepared to have me walk out on the sale if I don't give it to you?*

If you are still not convinced that you should divulge it:

> *Can I speak with the owner of the business, please?* (supervisor)
>
> *Does the Better Business Bureau agree with your right to require this information?*

In this situation, you are not preventing immediate identity theft. You are avoiding identity creep by only giving out the information that is actually necessary.

☐ A woman calls and says that she is from your credit card company. She believes that your card is being used fraudulently and she needs to ask you a couple of questions. What do you do?

> *Can I ask more questions about why you need this information?* (Ask why)
>
> *Can you verify the last three purchases I made on my account?* (Let's talk about me)
>
> *Can you tell me how long I have been a card member?*

Can I give you a call back using the number on my credit card? (Call them back)

☐ Someone comes into your business wearing the standard uniform of your regular computer technician but you don't recognize her. She has a plausible story and asks for access to your server.

Weren't you guys just in here yesterday? (Get her to lie)

Can I see your ID badge, please? (Verify identity)

Can you hold on a minute while I call to verify your credentials?

Who within our company ordered the service call?

☐ When you drive up to your ATM machine, there is a repairman there. He says that everything is ready to go; you just need to insert your card and get started.

You politely say, "No thank you," and find another ATM or go directly to the bank.

Know when to say no.

Early detection is the best way to keep the costs of identity theft to a minimum.

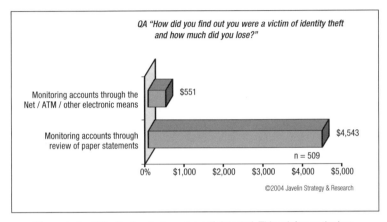

QA "How did you find out you were a victim of identity theft and how much did you lose?"

Monitoring accounts through the Net / ATM / other electronic means — $551

Monitoring accounts through review of paper statements — $4,543

n = 509

©2004 Javelin Strategy & Research

The majority of identity fraud crimes are self-detected. This reinforces the benefits of actively monitoring through electronic review of transactions, statements, and credit reports allowing consumers to check their account activities quickly and efficiently—without waiting for a paper bill or statement.[14]

10

The 7th Mindset— Plan B

Let's say that the enemy has gained access to your identity. Now what?

Stolen Life #3,392

Dixie's sister, Danny, came to live with her for the spring. Recently out of drug rehab, Danny didn't have a way to make ends meet and needed help getting back on her feet. Dixie, a deeply caring and religious person, decided to fill that role. It didn't take Danny long to "recover."

Danny began using drugs almost immediately after her release, stealing petty cash from Dixie's home that would never be missed. But this quickly ran out. Because she was in the house alone while Dixie was at work, Danny had access to virtually every document and piece of information in the house. Dixie and her husband took no special preventative steps to protect their sensitive information and Danny felt that this was careless of them. She felt that they were deliberately tempting her.

In April, Danny was able to look through the tax documents that were left on the office desk before being sealed and mailed. They contained everything Danny needed to set up accounts on Dixie's credit without ever alerting Dixie to the problem. Because they looked alike, it was simple for Danny to get a driver's license in Dixie's name. Danny was able to fully adopt an alternate identity without being detected. In most cases, detection would have taken years, as all of the accounts that Danny set up were entirely new and covered by Dixie's perfect credit.

Unknowingly, Dixie had a backup plan that would save her hours of recovery. Having read an article in the newspaper about getting a free annual credit report from each of the three credit bureaus, Dixie ordered her first copy in May. She was curious to see what a credit report looked like. And was she ever surprised to find out how much money she was spending!

Dixie alerted the credit bureaus the same day that she received her first credit report, followed the guidelines put out by the Federal Trade Commission for identity theft *victims and stopped her sister before she could make full use of Dixie's identity. Recovery took less than 30 hours and cost her $15 in notary fees.*

Prepare for the worst by having a backup plan—a way to detect fraud early in the game. **Develop a Plan B!**

"The fastest method to detect fraud is through self-detection by electronic means. Self-detection by electronic means [email or internet statements] resulted in lowest loss of money compared to other methods of detection."

—*The 2005 Identity Fraud Survey Report*, Javelin Strategy & Research

$ **Victims who monitored their accounts online detected fraud 6X faster than those using paper statements.**

Average Time to detect fraud (and resulting Average Fraud Amount) for victims using:

Paper statements: **114 days ($4,543)**

Electronic (internet/email) statements: **18 days ($551)**[9]

Spy Mindset: If anything can go wrong in the world of espionage, it will. Spies always prepare for the worst-case scenario by having a backup plan.

Plan B Mindset: In case our identity is stolen, we need a backup plan that will speed detection and minimize damage without a great deal of extra work.

It is just not possible to observe and ward off every threat to our identity. There will be documents that you forget to destroy or lock up, accounts that you won't cancel, checks that you will mail, and waiters that will disappear with your credit card. It is not practical to think that we can cover every situation that threatens the safety of our identity. And there are situations that are completely out of our control, like data loss by large companies. But we are not helpless in these situations.

Like an experienced spy, we have a solid backup plan. *Plan B* gives us a way to monitor the key components of our identity even as we accumulate, simplify, destroy, secure, observe, evaluate and interrogate. *Plan B* is our safety valve, and once implemented, it is simple and effective. It starts with a dossier.

> *If anything can go wrong, it will.*
>
> —Murphy's Law

A **dossier** (doss-e-ay) is nothing more than a collection of critical information on a single individual. It is like a report card on your credit identity. Unlike spies, who use dossiers to understand the people on whom they are spying, *you will be collecting information on yourself.*

☑ Action Items: Create a Dossier

Your dossier will be a collection of documents that are stored in your fire-safe and that you regularly review and update. It is a paper summary of your identity as the outside world sees it (businesses, organizations and governments). It is made up of several key documents: your credit report, bank and credit card statements, Social Security statement, wallet photocopies and your password list. Virtually any of your vital documents could be included in your dossier as well (birth certificates, marriage licenses, etc.).

A dossier has two purposes. First, it is a place where you can quickly access a complete record of your vital information in case your identity is stolen. You will have the necessary account and phone numbers at hand to cancel credit cards, bank accounts and to file credit disputes. And you can do it quickly.

> *Preparedness prevents peril.*
>
> Chinese Proverb

Second, by keeping the documents in a single place, you are able to compare them over time to spot changes or inconsistencies. For example, if you review your old credit history report and then the latest version, you will quickly spot any changes that have occurred.

☐ Buy a three ring binder. This will become your dossier. File the credit reports in the binder so you can refer back to them and compare the contents to your latest credit report. **Your dossier should be locked up in your fire-safe when you are not using it.**

☑ Action Items: Order and Monitor Your Credit Report

A credit report is a history of how you pay off your credit. There are currently three credit bureaus in the United States—Equifax, Experian and TransUnion. If you own a home, have a credit card, lease a car, or apply for or use credit of any sort, this information is reported to one, two or all three of these credit bureaus. In addition, they collect information on how timely you pay your bills, how often you are tardy, how frequently your credit is checked by companies and any changes of address, employment, or personal information.

By monitoring these reports closely, you will know when someone else is using your credit rating to their benefit. If an identity thief opens a new credit card or loan on your Social Security number, you will see it on your report. The quicker you spot the problem, the less trouble it will cause. **Monitoring your credit report is the single most effective tool available to keep minor identity theft from turning into full-scale identity fraud.**

☐ Order your credit report from the first of three agencies. By law, you are entitled to one free report from each agency once a year. The easiest way to get a report is to visit *www.annualcreditreport.com* or call 1-877-322-8228. Make sure that you request your free annual credit report from one credit agency only, as you will order the other two reports throughout the remainder of the year. By spreading the reports out over time, you will be monitoring your files consistently and frequently.

• Skip ahead 4 months from today on your calendar, and mark down the following information:

Request & Review Next Credit Report—
www.annualcreditreport.com or 1-877-322-8228.

• The second time you request your report, choose a credit agency that you didn't chose the first time (e.g., if you chose Equifax first, chose Experian second, TransUnion third and back to Equifax one year from today).

• Skip forward 8 and 12 months on your calendar and mark down which credit bureau you should request a credit report from. On month 12, you will be requesting the report from the same credit bureau that you requested it from the first time.

• If you use an electronic calendar, schedule this as a recurring event for every four months—that way you will be automatically reminded every time you should review your credit.

When you receive your first credit report, follow these steps:

☐ Completely read through the entire report and the definitions that the credit reporting agency gives you so you understand how to interpret the information. For a better understanding of how to interpret a credit report, read Appendix B, *Understanding Your Credit Report*.

☐ While reviewing your report a second time, use a highlighter to mark any accounts that you don't recognize or that appear to contain inaccurate information (e.g., negative credit feedback where there should be none), and a different colored highlighter for any accounts that you no longer need or use.

☐ Contact the credit bureau about any accounts that you have highlighted because you don't recognize them or because of erroneous information. Be aware that some companies give you a credit card with their name on it (like Sears) that is issued by another company (GE Capital). You may need to do some research on your credit card statements to understand who actually issued the card. The credit bureau should help you work through the questionable information.

☐ If the account appears to be one that you didn't authorize or set up, have the credit bureau put a temporary fraud alert on your account

(See more about fraud alerts in the next chapter). This will give you added protection from any additional fraud for 90 days while you determine what has happened. Follow the directions that come with your credit report. If you cannot find the directions, contact the appropriate credit bureau at the numbers or websites below:

- ☐ Equifax: *www.equifax.com*; 800-685-1111

- ☐ Experian: *www.experian.com*; 888-397-3742

- ☐ TransUnion: *www.transunion.com*; 800-916-8800

☐ Call and cancel all of the accounts on your credit report that you no longer need or use. Call one company per day until all of the accounts are cancelled. Make sure that you call the company that issued the card or loan, not the credit bureau.

For example, if you have five credit cards that you no longer need (and probably have forgotten you even had), call each credit card company, settle any balances and cancel the account. This is another means of *Simplifying your Identity* by means of *Accumulation*. It minimizes the number of places that a thief can take advantage of your credit.

☐ For the most protection and to make recovery a simple process, carry only one or two credit cards in your wallet. If you have more than this, you should ask yourself what purpose they are actually serving.

☐ The next time you review your report, you should look for any changes as compared to the previous report. If there are changes, make sure that it is credit that you applied for, and not a new account set up by an identity thief. You will probably have very little work to do on future versions of your credit report as most of the hard work is done on the first round. Use this first time to educate yourself about credit reports and to clean up the years of neglect and identity creep.

☐ Make sure to have your spouse or partner order and monitor their credit reports, as they are mostly independent of yours.

Consider Credit Monitoring Services & Identity Theft Insurance

☐ To detect many types of identity fraud in the earliest stages (and therefore minimize damage even further), you can subscribe to one of the credit monitoring services provided by all three credit bureaus. For a monthly or yearly fee, the agency of your choice will notify you by email of any changes or activity in your credit reports. Most of these services come with identity theft insurance as well as the reports. Some of the bureaus even offer a 3-in-1 monitoring service that alerts you to changes in any of the 3 bureaus' reports. The services are somewhat costly, but will alert you very quickly if there is activity in your account.

I recommend these services for people who are either too busy to regularly check their credit reports (and have an extra $120 per year to spend), would like the extra peace of mind, or people who are already victims of identity theft. This is an easy way to track whether or not identity thieves are still taking advantage of your good name.

Identity theft insurance is offered by many insurance companies as an endorsement on your homeowner's policy. They tend to be relatively inexpensive and cover many of the fees associated with identity theft recovery. The biggest recovery expense is usually the legal fees necessary to recover your credit and fight any criminal actions. Every company's policy is slightly different, so make sure that you understand which legal fees are covered and which are not.

Monitor Your Monthly Statements

Bank, credit card, debit card and brokerage statements give a transaction by transaction replay of where you spent your money for the month. The more often you monitor them, the more quickly you will detect foul play.

☐ If possible, monitor your statements online. This has two benefits. First, it removes the paper statements from the mail. Second, because there is very little lag time between making a charge on your card and being able to view it online, you cut down detection time significantly. This is how people keep identity fraud from spinning out of control.

If this isn't possible, review them as they arrive in the mail. If you are receiving paper bills, consider the following tip:

Use an electronic calendar (like Microsoft Outlook) to track your billing cycles. Since most statements arrive at about the same time each month, put a reminder in your calendar to watch for the statement in the mail. Use the recurring events feature in your Outlook to remind you of the statement every month. If the statement doesn't show up on time, call the company that issued the statement and ask when it was mailed.

☐ Several credit card companies have alert features that will notify you when certain conditions are met regarding your account. For example, BankOne (now Chase) has customer alerts that will email you every time a transaction is made, a payment is due or is not received by Chase, and many other criteria. This is a phenomenally easy way to keep track of credit card usage. If you haven't used your credit card and you receive an alert, you have an immediate form of detecting identity theft.

☐ Review every transaction on the statement and make sure that you recognize where the charge is coming from and that the amount is correct or at least reasonable. Remember that identity thieves are usually smart enough to charge small amounts (or write small checks) each month because they are harder to detect.

☐ If you find a discrepancy, immediately file a dispute with the credit card company or bank. If it turns out to be legitimate, you can always remove the dispute. In the meantime, protect yourself.

☐ You probably won't file your individual statements in your dossier (there would be too many), but it is a good place to file end-of-year statements and summaries.

Monitor Your Annual Social Security Statement

☐ Every year you receive an account statement from the Social Security Administration. It details your yearly earning record, expected retirement benefits, and disability benefits. If your Social Security number has been stolen and someone is taking advantage of your benefits, you should be able to detect it by monitoring any changes in the statements. Make sure that your yearly Earnings Record on the statement matches your taxable income on your tax return. Verify that your benefits are increasing each year as you contribute more to retirement, not decreasing because someone is prematurely redeeming them.

☐ Make sure to have your spouse or partner monitor his or her Social Security Statement as it is completely independent of yours.

☐ Keep these statements in your dossier, or with that year's taxes.

Make Photocopies and Logs

☐ In Chapter 5, *Simplify Your Identity*, you made a copy of every piece of identity in your wallet. This copy should be stored in your dossier (which is kept in your fire-safe) and updated anytime there are significant changes. This document allows you to quickly find and contact credit card companies, motor vehicle departments, banks and other institutions that should be alerted if your wallet is lost or stolen.

☐ As you opt-out of marketing lists and information sharing, add the documents to your dossier for future reference and verification. Keep a to-do list at the start of your dossier to track any future action items and the dates they need to be performed. For example, many of the opt-out programs only last for five years and need to be renewed. Write yourself a note on this page and include the date when you should renew your request.

☐ Make a log of all of the important accounts, account numbers, login names and passwords for every account you have. This should include bank accounts, brokerage accounts, insurance accounts, utilities and phone accounts and any other financial institutions that require passwords or PIN numbers on their website, phone system or ATM. If your identity is stolen, you will have all of the accounts in a convenient and safe place for quick access. It also provides a centralized place for your spouse to find financial information if something should happen to you.

Freeze Your Credit—The Quickest Fix

☐ Several states allow you to "freeze" your credit and many more are jumping on the bandwagon. If your state is one of them, I highly recommend that you participate. To find out if your state participates, visit: *www.consumersunion.org/campaigns/learn_more/002355indiv.html*

A security freeze gives you the power to prevent anyone from looking at your credit file unless you choose to allow them access. This gives you control over who can access your private information and effectively prevents identity thieves from opening new accounts in your name. In most states it costs about $10 anytime you want to "unfreeze" your report.

> ALONG WITH BUYING THIS BOOK, A PAPER SHREDDER, A FIRE-SAFE, A DOSSIER NOTEBOOK AND COMPUTER SECURITY, THIS IS THE MOST WORTHWHILE MONEY YOU WILL SPEND PROTECTING YOUR IDENTITY.

Temporarily reversing your credit freeze can be inconvenient, but this serves as a reminder to keep your identity simple. You won't be signing up for any accounts that you don't absolutely need. To unfreeze your credit during a transaction (e.g., when you are applying for a car or home loan), you simply contact the credit bureau (you are initiating the contact), give them your password, and ask them to temporarily unfreeze your credit.

☐ Store your credit freeze documents in your dossier so that you have easy access to them if you want to unfreeze your credit.

11

Recovering from Identity Theft— the Basics

This section lists only the first and most crucial steps you must take if you are a victim of identity theft. It is important that you consult other resources and take more detailed action. I recommend that you take the steps below first and then visit the Recovery Websites listed in Appendix A for further steps.

The Top 12 Ways Victims Detect Identity Theft

1. Your bills or statements are not arriving in your mail on time.

2. You notice unauthorized charges on your credit card bill.

3. You notice new accounts or erroneous information on your credit report.

4. You are denied credit for a large purchase.

5. You receive credit card bills from cards you don't own.

6. You are contacted by a collection agency on an item you didn't purchase.

7. You receive bills for unknown purchases.

8. You are unable to set up new banking, loan or brokerage accounts.

9. You notice withdrawals on your checking or savings account that you didn't make.

10. The checks listed on your bank statements don't reconcile with those listed in your check register. Many times these checks are made out to "Cash."

11. You notice a downward trend in benefits on your Annual Social Security Statement.

12. The police show up at your door.

☑ Action Items: Take Action Now

As you take the following steps, you should keep a log of every step you have taken, who you spoke with, the date and time of your conversation and the results of your call. This log of contacts will become part of your dossier and will help you prove your financial, civil and criminal innocence, should they be questioned.

☐ **Contact the Credit Bureaus.** Immediately place a fraud alert with all three credit reporting bureaus. A fraud alert requests that creditors contact you before issuing credit or opening new accounts in your name. If you report it to one bureau, they are supposed to report it to the other two. However, this could take days, so I would report it to each agency separately just to be safe.

   ☐ Equifax: 1-800-525-6285 or *www.equifax.com*.

   ☐ Experian: 1-888-397-3742 *www.experian.com*.

   ☐ TransUnion: 1-800-680-7289 or *www.transunion.com*.

Here is what you should discuss with each bureau:

• Your identity is being used by another person to fraudulently obtain credit in your name.

• Ask them to place a Fraud Alert on your credit file. This is temporary and will last for 90-180 days only.

• Have them add a victim's statement to your report that reads "My ID has been stolen and used to fraudulently apply for credit. Please call me at [your phone number—cell phones are generally best because you carry them with you] to verify all applications."

• Verify with the bureau that you will be receiving a current copy of your credit report as well as instructions on how to file an extended seven-year fraud alert.

☐ **Contact New Creditors.** You should immediately contact all new creditors that have been set up fraudulently. If the identity thief took out a home loan, call the loan agency and alert them to the problem. Request that they close the account immediately. They may ask for supporting documents such as fraud affidavits and police reports (discussed below).

If credit card accounts have been opened in your name, call the credit card issuer and tell them that you have been the victim of identity theft. Ask to close the account and have all fraudulent charges removed. Make sure that you follow up with the creditors to verify that all fraudulent accounts have been closed. Don't count on them to do everything you request without supervision.

If you are contacted by debt collectors, respond immediately in writing and keep a copy of your letter. Explain that you are the victim of identity theft and that you don't owe the money. You have the right to ask the debt collector for the name of the business that is owed the debt. Include your theft or fraud affidavit and a copy of the police report with your letter.

☐ **Contact Existing Creditors.** If the thief is using your existing accounts (credit cards, lines of credit, etc), contact each company and have your old accounts closed. Request that they tag the accounts with "Account closed at consumer's request" so that it is clear that you were not at fault. Make sure that you add a password to all existing accounts to provide an additional layer of security.

If your checks, credit cards or debit cards have been lost or stolen, call each bank/company immediately and cancel the accounts. All of this information should be located in your dossier. Set up new account numbers with new passwords (according to the password criteria outlined in Chapter 7, *Secure the Essentials*). For bank accounts, you will probably have to visit your local branch to cancel the old accounts and set up the new. Don't delay in getting this done as the bank only covers theft that is reported in a "reasonable" time.

For credit cards, under federal law, you are only responsible for a maximum of $50 if you report the fraudulent charges immediately.

☐ **Contact the Check Verification Companies.** If your checks were stolen or new checking accounts were established in your name, call the check verification companies and report the fraudulent checks:

    ☐ Chexsystems: 1-800-428-9623

    ☐ CheckCenter/CrossCheck:1-800-843-0760

    ☐ Certigy/Equifax: 1-800-437-5120

    ☐ International Check Services: 1-800-526-5380

    ☐ SCAN: 1-800-262-7771

    ☐ Telecheck: 1-800-710-9898

☐ **File a Police Report.** Immediately report the crime to your local police department. The chances that they will pursue the criminal are small, but you need a copy of the police report to begin proving your innocence to creditors and law enforcement agencies. Some law enforcement agencies see so much identity theft that they make filling out a report quite a chore for the victim. Stick with it until you have a legitimate report. Make sure that you:

• Include the fraudulent account numbers in the report that were established.

• Include any and all documented proof you have that the accounts are fraudulent.

• Include any information that you have on the thief or the crime.

• Get a copy of the report; you will need it repeatedly while straightening out your credit and legal issues.

☐ **Fill out an ID Theft Affidavit.** The FTC makes a copy of this available at *www.ftc.gov/bcp/conline/pubs/credit/affidavit.pdf.* You will use this document repeatedly in the next few weeks.

☐ **Extend Your Fraud Alerts with the Credit Bureaus.** After you receive the credit reports, follow the instructions from each bureau on how to extend the length of your fraud alert for a period of 7 years rather than 90 days. You will generally have to do this in writing, and may need to include supporting documentation such as a fraud affidavit or police report. Make sure you reference the unique ID number that the bureau assigns your case, and use certified, return receipt mail when you send the requests. This is how you will know that they are processing your request and that action is being taken. Fraud alerts can be removed from your account at any time.

Some of the items you should request in your written letters to each bureau are:

• Ask for the names and phone numbers of the credit grantors that were fraudulently established by the identity thief. This will save you time researching contact information.

• Request that the bureaus remove inquiries on your account that are due to the fraudulent activities.

• In some states, the bureaus are required to remove fraudulent accounts if you include a copy of the police report with your request. Ask them if you are one of these states.

• Ask the bureaus to notify any companies that have received your erroneous credit reports in the past few months to alert them to the disputed information.

• When you have been granted an extended alert, you are allowed two free copies of everything in your credit file over the first 12 months. Take advantage of the second report to make sure that you have cleared everything to your satisfaction.

Please be aware that these measures will not necessarily stop new fraudulent accounts from being established by the identity thief. Credit issuers (credit card companies, car dealers, lending companies, etc.) are not required by law to observe fraud alerts. Consequently, you should monitor your credit report from this point on with increased diligence to spot any suspicious activity.

☐ **Go to the FTC website.** Visit *www.consumer.gov/idtheft/* to file an identity theft report and to verify that you have taken all of the steps suggested by the Federal Trade Commission.

☐ **Notify the Postal Inspector.** If you feel that you are the victim of mail theft or a fraudulent change of address, contact the Postal Inspector's Office. Call the U.S. Post Office at 1-800-275-8777 to obtain your regional number.

☐ **Contact the Social Security Administration.** If your Social Security Number has been stolen and is being used to commit benefits or unemployment fraud, contact the SSA. They can be reached at *www.ssa.gov.*

☐ **Contact the Passport Office.** Whether you have a passport or not, alert the passport office to warn them about fraudulent passport applications in your name.

☐ **Secure your Phone Service.** Call your phone companies (local, cell and long distance) and ask them to password protect your account.

☐ **Protect your Driver's License.** If someone is using your driver's license number to write bad checks, contact your state's Department of Motor Vehicles to see if another license has been issued in your name. Have them place a fraud alert on your license if possible. If not, ask them the procedure in your state for filing a complaint.

12

Your Calendar of Prevention

This section lists all the Action Items that are important to take to protect your identity. They are organized by priority. The steps that I consider to be the most important appear first, and so on. I determined the priority of action items according to three questions:

1. Which actions most drastically reduce your statistical chances of becoming a victim of identity theft?

2. If identity theft cannot be avoided, which actions provide the most effective damage control to minimize your costs and exposure?

3. Which items are you most likely to complete due to effort levels and the time commitment required to protect your identity?

> **Note:** All the information you need to take steps to prevent identity theft is contained in this section. If you skipped the chapters and did not read about the Mindsets and how to establish habits of security, you still will be able to protect yourself by following each step listed below. I strongly recommend you go back when you can and read about how to make identity prevention a way of life. Identity theft is not going to go away.
>
> If you have already completed the tasks as you read the chapters, skim this section for any Action Items that you might have missed. And don't forget, protecting yourself does not stop here. Make a daily habit of privacy and of thinking like a spy when your identity is involved.

I highly recommend that you set up a schedule for yourself. Be flexible. Take ten minutes a day or one hour a week or one weekend a month and schedule time to "accumulate privacy." If you have to wait on one of the action items, e.g., you order your credit report but it takes ten days to receive, move on to one of the items further down the list and then go back when you receive the report.

When your interest in protecting your greatest financial asset (your identity) begins to weaken, remember that your chances of becoming a victim of identity theft are 1-in-10 over the next two years. The average cost to a victim is over $5,600 and the amount of time spent recovering is immense. This is no time to lose sight of the goal. When you complete these items, your risk of identity theft should be less than 1% or 1 in 100.

I wish I were able to guarantee that completing these action items and reading this book would protect you 100%. But it won't. There is no fail-safe against any crime, only ways to better protect yourself. Consider these exercises as the locks, alarms and watchdogs of your identity.

Step 1: Freeze Your Credit—The Quickest Fix

Several states allow you to "freeze" your credit and many more are jumping on the bandwagon. If your state is one of them, I highly recommend that you participate. To find out if your state participates, visit: *www.consumersunion.org/campaigns/learn_more/002355indiv.html*

A security freeze gives you the power to prevent anyone from looking at your credit file unless you choose to allow them access. This gives you control over who can access your private information and effectively prevents identity thieves from opening new accounts in your name. In most states it costs about $10 anytime you want to "unfreeze" your report. ALONG WITH BUYING THIS BOOK, A PAPER SHREDDER, A FIRE-SAFE, A DOSSIER NOTEBOOK AND COMPUTER SECURITY, THIS IS THE MOST WORTHWHILE MONEY YOU WILL SPEND PROTECTING YOUR IDENTITY.

To unfreeze your credit during a transaction, you simply contact the credit bureau, give them your password (you are initiating the contact, so concerns over ID theft are lessened), and ask them to temporarily unfreeze your credit.

Store your credit freeze documents in your dossier (see page 117) so that you have easy access to them if you want to unfreeze your credit.

Step 2: Order Your Credit Report

A credit report is a history of how you pay off your credit. There are currently three credit bureaus in the United States—Equifax, Experian and TransUnion. If you own a home, have a credit card, lease a car, or apply for or use credit of any sort, your use of credit is reported to one, two or all three of these credit bureaus. In addition, they collect information on how timely you pay your bills, how often you are tardy, how frequently your credit is checked by companies and any changes of address, employment or personal information.

By monitoring these reports closely, you will know when someone else is using your credit rating to their benefit. If an identity thief opens a new credit card or loan on your Social Security number, you will see it on your report. The quicker you spot the problem, the less trouble it will cause. **Monitoring your credit report is the single most effective tool available to keep minor identity theft from turning into full-scale identity fraud.**

☐ **Order your credit report from the first of three agencies.** By law, you are entitled to one free report from each agency once a year. The easiest way to get a report is to visit *www.annualcreditreport.com* or call 1-877-322-8228. You also can contact the agencies individually.

Equifax: *www.equifax.com*; 800-685-1111

Experian: *www.experian.com*; 888-397-3742

TransUnion: *www.transunion.com*; 800-916-8800

Make sure that you request your free annual credit report from one credit agency at a time, as you will order the other two reports throughout the remainder of the year. By spreading the reports out over time, you will be monitoring your files consistently and frequently.

- Skip ahead four months from today on your calendar, and mark down the following information:

  Request & Review Next Credit Report—
  www.annualcreditreport.com or 1-877-322-8228.

- The second time you request your report, choose a credit agency that you didn't choose the first time.

- Skip forward eight and twelve months on your calendar and mark down which credit bureau you should request a credit report from. On month twelve, you will be requesting the report from the same credit bureau that you requested it from the first time.

- If you use an electronic calendar, schedule this as a recurring event for every four months—that way you will be automatically reminded.

☐ Buy a three-ring binder. This will become your dossier. File the credit reports in the binder so that you can refer back to them and compare the contents to your latest credit report. Your dossier should be locked up in your fire-safe when you are not using it.

☐ **Look into Credit Monitoring Services**. For an added level of protection, look into a subscription to one of the credit monitoring services provided by all three credit bureaus. The monitoring services speed up the detection time of many types of identity fraud (and therefore minimize damage even further). For a monthly or yearly fee, the agency of your choice will notify you by email of any changes or activity in your credit reports. Most of these services come with identity theft insurance as well as the reports. Some of the bureaus even offer a 3-in-1 monitoring service that alerts you to changes in any of the three bureaus' reports. The services are somewhat costly, but will alert you very quickly if there is activity in your account.

I recommend these services for people who are too busy to regularly check their credit reports (and have an extra $120 per year to spend), would like the extra peace of mind, or are already victims of identity theft. This is an easy way to track whether or not identity thieves are still taking advantage of your good name.

Step 3: Review Your Credit Report for Signs of Theft or Fraud

☐ Once you receive your first credit report, read through the entire report and the definitions that the credit reporting agency gives you so that you understand how to interpret the information. For a better understanding of how to interpret a credit report, read Appendix B, *Understanding Your Credit Report.*

☐ While reviewing your report a second time, use a highlighter to mark any accounts that you don't recognize or that appear to contain inaccurate information (e.g., negative credit feedback where there should be none), and a different colored highlighter for any accounts that you no longer need or use.

Step 4: Resolve Issues on Your Credit Report

☐ Contact the credit bureau about any accounts that you have highlighted because you don't recognize them or because of erroneous information. Be aware that some companies give you a credit card with their name on it (like Sears) that is issued by another company (GE Capital). You may need to do some research on your credit card statements to understand who actually issued the card. The credit bureau should help you work through the questionable information.

☐ If the account appears to be one that you didn't authorize or set up, have the credit bureau put a temporary fraud alert on your account. This will give you added protection from any additional fraud for 90 days while you determine what has happened. Follow the directions that come with your credit report. If you cannot find the directions, contact the appropriate credit bureau at the numbers or websites below:

> Equifax: *www.equifax.com*; 800-685-1111
>
> Experian: *www.experian.com*; 888-397-3742
>
> TransUnion: *www.transunion.com*; 800-916-8800

If your identity has been stolen, please also read Chapter 11, *Recovering From Identity Theft.*

Step 5: Simplify Your Credit Report by Canceling Unnecessary Accounts

☐ Call and cancel all of the accounts on your credit report that you no longer need or use. Call one company per day until all of the accounts are cancelled. Make sure that you call the company that issued the card or loan, not the credit bureau.

☐ The next time you review your report, you should look for any changes as compared to the previous report. If there are changes, make sure that it is credit that you applied for, and not a new account set up by an identity thief. You will probably have very little work to do on future versions of your credit report as most of the hard work is done on the first round. Use this first time to educate yourself about credit reports and to clean up the years of neglect and identity creep (the slow and unnecessary leakage of our personal information).

☐ Make sure to have your spouse or partner order and monitor their credit reports, as theirs are mostly independent of yours.

Step 6: Protect Your Wallet and/or Purse by Removing Unnecessary Items

A lost or stolen wallet, purse, checkbook or credit card accounts for 29% of identity theft[4]. That means we can prevent a pretty large piece of the identity theft pie if we simply protect our wallets. But this isn't always possible, so we must minimize damage if it does fall into the wrong hands. The fewer pieces of identity you have in your wallet, the less susceptible you are to theft and the easier it is to recover if you suddenly become a victim. Just as a spy prepares himself in case he falls into the hands of the enemy, you should be prepared for your wallet or purse to end up in the hands of a thief.

Remove the following items from your wallet or purse:

☐ **Social Security Card.** You should only need this in rare circumstances (e.g., your first day on the job). If stolen, it can be used to set up new credit card accounts, driver's licenses, loans and bank accounts. It can also be used to steal your retirement benefits, draw unemployment or take out bankruptcy. Your Social Security number is one piece of your identity that you should protect fiercely. File your card in a fire-safe as discussed in *Securing the Essentials*.

☐ **Checks.** Check fraud is one of the largest and easiest forms of identity theft. Stop carrying checks and use your credit card, debit card or cash. If you can't survive without checks, carry them only when you go shopping, and make sure that your account has as little in it as possible (transfer any excess into your savings until you need it). Don't make excuses for skipping this task—it could have very negative consequences.

• Carrying only one check in your purse or wallet doesn't help much. It is not just the physical check that the thief is looking for, but the account and bank routing numbers on the bottom of the check that allow them to make duplicate checks or access the account electronically.

• Make sure that you don't have your SSN, driver's license number or home phone number on your checks. It is preferable to use a work address and phone number, which doesn't lead back to your home. Some people advise that you have your first and middle initial printed on the check instead of your full name. This does a good job of concealing your name, but most banks don't verify signatures on checks less than $3,000 anyway, so it probably won't stop fraud.

• Never put full account numbers or Social Security numbers on the Notes line of your check. Use the lasts four digits only—banks and credit card companies can identify you from these numbers.

• Make sure to always sign your checks (and vital documents) with a felt-tip or pigmented ink-pen (like a uni-ball® 207™ gel pen) or permanent marker (like a Sharpie®). This helps prevent theives from "lifting" the ink from checks, mortgages and other vital documents.

☐ **PIN Numbers and Passwords.** Remove all passwords and PIN numbers from your purse or wallet for bank accounts, websites, debit cards, computers, home alarms, garage doors, etc. See Chapter 7, *Secure the Essentials* for an easy way to create and remember passwords so that you won't have to carry them with you.

☐ **Excess Credit and Debit Cards.** We tend to collect credit cards and bank accounts even though we don't need them (usually because we received a short-term bribe for signing up). Remove them from your wallet and then cancel all of these accounts. If possible, carry no more than two cards in your wallet. This makes post-theft recovery much easier and less time-consuming.

☐ **Credit Card Receipts.** File them securely if you need them for tax purposes or expense tracking. Otherwise, destroy them. To learn about how best to destroy documents, credit cards, CD-ROMs, and other forms of identity, please visit Chapter 6, *Destroy Private Information*. You will find more information on what to lock up and how to secure your documents when you read Chapter 7, *Secure the Essentials*.

☐ **ATM Receipts and Bank Deposit Slips.** Record the transactions and shred them once they have cleared your bank.

Step 7: Remove All Forms of Your Social Security Number from Your Wallet

☐ **Driver's License.** In many states, SSNs appear on your driver's license. Most states will allow you to keep it off of your card, but it may require getting a new driver's license. It is worth the trouble.

☐ **Medical Cards.** SSNs are often printed on medical insurance or HMO/PPO cards. In many states, the insurance company is required to send you a new card with a non-SSN identification number if requested. Make the request.

☐ **Student ID Cards.** Many colleges and universities use your SSN as a student ID number. Request a new card with a different method of identification.

☐ **Military ID/Government Cards.** Many government-issued cards use your SSN for identification. Some branches of the military require you to carry your card at all times, in which case you are out of luck. Check with your specific agency or branch to find out if you must carry your card at all times. Otherwise, carry it only when necessary.

Step 8: Prepare to Have Your Wallet or Purse Lost or Stolen

☐ **Signature & "Photo ID Required."** Sign your credit cards with *both your signature and "Photo ID Required."* Also, write the same message on the front of the card with indelible ink (since most stores don't even look at your signature on the back). It can be removed somewhat easily, but it helps discourage thieves as they know you are watching out for identity theft.

Please be aware that you need to *sign your name on the back of the card* to be in compliance with many credit card company contracts. Without your signature, some of them are able to deny any claims of fraud and refuse to reimburse what was stolen. Don't simply put "Photo ID Required."

☐ **Photocopy.** Make a photocopy (front and back) of every piece of identity that stays in your wallet. If it is lost or stolen, this will make it easy to call the companies and cancel your cards, accounts, etc. File it in your dossier.

☐ **From today on, make your wallet a sacred place.** Don't add information to it unless it is absolutely necessary. Use it as a control point to stop identity creep. Lock it up at the gym (in private) and don't leave it exposed in your car or at work.

☐ Don't forget to have your spouse or partner follow the same steps to protect his or her wallet or purse.

Step 9: Stop Paying Bills by Check

One of the best ways to prevent identity theft is to stop using the mail. Several alternate methods of paying bills are available.

☐ **Auto-Pay.** Set up auto-pay by credit card. You can generally do this with most major companies (phone bill, utilities, cable TV, insurance, etc.). You can also pay by credit card on a month-by-month basis on most websites. This isn't as convenient, but gives you more control over your charges. I like this option the best as it gives you an easy method to dispute charges (you call the credit card company and freeze the payment until your dispute is settled). In addition, your liability is only $50 if you report fraud in a reasonable time frame.

☐ **Electronic Funds Transfer.** Since you cannot pay a credit card with a credit card (well, technically you can, but we won't go into that), you will have to pay by other means. You can set up an electronic funds transfer between your bank and the bank of the company you owe money. For example, many insurance agencies don't allow credit card payments, but will automatically deduct your premium each month directly from your bank account. I use this option if the credit card option is not available and if I trust the company who will be withdrawing the funds.

☐ **Bill Pay.** You can use an electronic bill-payment service, which is offered by most banks, brokerages and many other sources. This is a good third option. Most of the electronic bill-payment services still cut paper checks and send them through the mail. This reduces the risk that an outgoing check will be stolen from your mailbox, but not the risk of it being stolen from the bill-payers mail, or in transit.

Step 10: Rotate Your Credit Cards

☐ If you have been a victim of data loss (where your private data is lost or stolen as happened recently with DSW, ChoicePoint, LexisNexis, etc.) or just want to "outdate" your credit card identity, once a year cancel the cards you do keep. Call each credit card company, cancel your existing card and have them issue a new card with a new credit card number. This means that all of those companies that have your credit card on file now have old data. And now that you have opted out of a great deal of information sharing, your new card number won't be in as many databases.

☐ Make sure you have any frequent flyer miles transferred to your new card number, or have your frequent flyer number attached to the new card. You don't want to lose miles just because you are being diligent.

☐ Don't forget to call any companies that have your credit card number on file for auto-pay (AOL, phone bill, electricity, etc.) and let them know your new number. Anyone who tries to use the old number will draw blanks. This measure isn't to protect against money loss (you only have a $50 liability on any credit card if you report it as lost or stolen in their "acceptable" time frame). It's to protect against the time involved if your credit card number is stolen.

Step 11: Pay with Cash

☐ If you are ever uncomfortable with giving out a check or your credit card, pay with cash. This old-fashioned way of paying has *absolutely zero identity creep*. Pay with cash when you don't want to share information that will ultimately be stored in a database and sold to other businesses. Companies buy your credit card histories so they can market other services to you. For example, certain businesses know that if you shop at a particular store, you are likely to buy their product.

Step 12: Eliminate Paper Statements that Arrive in the Mail

☐ Replace paper statements that arrive through the mail and sit out on desks with online statements that are automatically stored in your computer. The Better Business Bureau's first recommendation for the prevention of identity theft is to move to online statements and bill paying[12]. By replacing paper bills, statements and checks with paperless versions (on the internet), you eliminate the risk of having them stolen out of your mailbox.

☐ The next time you receive a statement of any kind in the mail, call the customer service number on the statement and ask them to move you to electronic statements. Make sure that they stop your paper statements. Over the course of a month, you should have moved almost every statement from paper to electronic. Don't forget to opt-out of information sharing while you are on the phone with them.

☐ Review and store your statements on your computer if possible. It will be much safer there (especially once you have read *Securing the Essentials*) than receiving them through the mail and storing them in a file cabinet. If you don't use a computer, read the section on securing your mail in *Securing the Essentials*.

☐ Most electronic statements come in the form of an Adobe Acrobat (or PDF) file. These can be saved directly to your hard drive in a folder named for their specific purpose (e.g., 2005 Schwab Statements—Account 4299).

☐ When you are online with your first statement, set up auto-alerts (if the company offers them) that alert you to any major activity on the account. For example, with E★Trade you can set up auto alerts that email you when certain transactions occur on your account. This is a great way to monitor your finances on a daily basis without much time investment. These same alerts are available on some credit cards, like those offered by BankOne (which is now Chase).

Step 13: Secure Your Mail

Stop using the mail to send and receive identity documents. This is the best solution (as described in the computer section) but not always possible. Therefore, here are alternative suggestions:

☐ **Lock Box.** Install a locking mailbox that can be accessed only by you. These generally have a mail slot that allows the postal service to put mail into the box.

☐ **P.O. Box.** If a locking mailbox is not possible, get a P.O. box at your local post office and have sensitive documents sent there. It is a little bit more work, but gives you much more privacy.

☐ **Hand Deliver.** When mailing sensitive documents, walk them into the post office and hand them to a postal worker. If it is after hours, drop the mail through an internal slot in the building. If there is no internal mailing slot, mail it the following day. This cuts out the most vulnerable stages of mailing.

☐ **UPS/FedEx.** Have identity documents sent by UPS or FedEx and require a signature for delivery. This makes the information harder to steal and you can track its location at anytime, which will alert you if the document isn't delivered in a timely manner or is diverted somewhere else.

☐ **Send to Bank.** Have sensitive documents (like new checks or credit cards) sent to your bank rather than to your home address. Pick them up there.

☐ **Monitor the Mail.** When new credit cards are coming through the mail, watch for them and call the credit card company if they don't arrive in 7 to10 days.

☐ **Quick Retrieval.** If you are unable to install a locking mailbox and don't have access to P.O. boxes, retrieve any mail within an hour or two of delivery. This lowers the exposure time of your mail.

☐ Review Chapter 5, *Simplify Your Identity* for tips on cutting down the amount of mail that arrives at your home.

Step 14: Monitor Your Monthly Statements

Bank, credit card, debit card and brokerage statements give a transaction by transaction replay of where you spent your money for the month. The more often you monitor them, the more quickly you will detect foul play.

☐ **Monitor Online.** If possible, monitor your statements online. This has two benefits. First, it removes the paper statements from the mail, which is a frequent target of identity thieves. Second, because there is very little lag time between making a charge on your card and being able to view it online, you cut down detection time significantly. This is how people keep identity fraud from spinning out of control.

If this isn't possible, review them as they arrive in the mail. If you are receiving paper bills, consider the following tip:

• Use an electronic calendar (like Microsoft Outlook) to track your billing cycles. Since most statements arrive at about the same time each month, put a reminder in your calendar to watch for the statement in the mail. Use the recurring events feature in your Outlook to remind you of the statement every month. If the statement doesn't show up on time, call the company that issued the statement and ask when it was mailed.

☐ **Set up Alerts.** Several credit card companies have alert features that will notify you when certain conditions are met regarding your account. For example, BankOne (now Chase) has customer alerts that will email you every time a transaction is made, a payment is due or is not received by Chase, and many other criteria. This is a phenomenally easy way to keep track of credit card usage. If you haven't used your credit card and you receive an alert, you have an immediate form of detecting identity theft.

☐ **Review Statements.** Review every transaction on the statement and make sure that you recognize where the charge is coming from and that the amount is correct or at least reasonable. Remember that identity thieves are usually smart enough to charge small amounts (or write small checks) each month because they are harder to detect.

• If you find a discrepancy, immediately file a dispute with the credit card company or bank. If it turns out to be legitimate, you can always remove the dispute. In the meantime, protect yourself.

• You probably won't file your individual statements in your dossier (there would be too many), but it is a good place to file end-of-year statements and summaries.

Step 15: Opt-Out of Pre-screened Credit Offers

☐ Opt-out of pre-screened credit offers, which are frequently stolen from mailboxes. Opting out means to remove yourself from their marketing lists. Pre-screened credit offers are when companies check your credit history with one of the three credit bureaus prior to sending you an offer for more credit (based on your good history). This could be a pre-approved credit card, loan or line of credit, etc. Call 1-888-5OPTOUT (1-888-567-8688) or visit *www.optoutprescreen.com.* Because the credit is pre-approved, it is a very attractive target for an identity thief.

Step 16: Purchase a Document Shredder and Fire-Safe

Go to your local office supply store and purchase the following items, or visit *www.thinklikeaspy.com* for our reviews on current shredders and safes.

☐ **Paper shredder.** This will be used to destroy historical documents as well as unnecessary junk mail. I recommend a cross-cut confetti shredder.

☐ **Fire-safe or fire-rated filing cabinet for your home.** This is where you will store your essential identity documents. Save money by purchasing a filing cabinet that is also fire-rated and eliminates the need for a fire-safe and a locking filing cabinet.

Step 17: Destroy Documents Containing Private Information

Place the shredder near to where you open mail or file documents so that you shred what would have normally been thrown away. Make sure that the shredder isn't where small children can get to it. If you don't want to buy a shredder, make sure you tear the documents into small pieces.

Here is a simple rule of thumb for what to destroy: anything with a piece of identity on it that will be thrown out with the trash, left in someone else's control or that can't be locked up. If you are leaving your identity in someone else's hands (the trash collector, the waiter, the sales clerk), your risk of identity theft just escalated. This should trigger alarms and cause you to think twice about leaving your information alone.

For a list of some of the most vulnerable items that go out in the trash and are good candidates for the shredder, refer back to Chapter 3.

Note: The best way to determine what historical financial documents to destroy is by asking your tax accountant or lawyer.

☐ Start shredding any papers that are going in the trash. Be generous with what you shred—overcompensating won't hurt you (unless you shred something you need).

☐ As you file your latest statements, cancelled checks, tax information, etc., decide if it is time to destroy the outdated copies of these documents.

☐ Use your new shredder as a reason to clean off the piles of identity on your desk, in your files, and throughout the house. Remember, 50% of identity theft is committed by someone who the victim knows[15]. Identity theft inside of the home is often committed by domestic help, contracted workers, guests and even friends and family.

☐ Before selling or donating your computer, make sure you have formatted the hard drive so that your data cannot be reconstructed. If you are throwing away or selling a cell phone, make sure you clean off all of your contacts and information first.

☐ If you own a business, make sure to destroy sensitive documents prior to discarding them to decrease your legal liability.

Effective June 1, 2005, businesses are required to destroy all consumer information before discarding it in the trash. The Fair & Accurate Credit Transaction Act (FACTA) Disposal Rule states that "any person who maintains or otherwise possesses consumer information for a business purpose" **must properly destroy the information prior to disposal**. FACTA further states that every person and/or business must take "reasonable measures" to protect against unauthorized access to the use of the information in connection with its disposal.

☐ When you are in a restaurant or retail store, I recommend that you scratch out all but the last four digits on the merchant copy of your credit card receipt. They have already processed the number electronically and should not be storing a paper copy of your number and expiration date. Tear up your copy if you don't need it for your records. Tear up any carbon paper if they are using manual swipe receipts.

Step 18: Protect Your Computer

It's a good idea to hire a professional computer technician. Make sure you are using a reputable company that has been around long enough to prove that they are honest.

Consider the expense money well spent. You will be securing thousands of dollars worth of data and significantly reducing your chances of identity theft in the process. A stolen Social Security number, which links to your retirement benefits and available credit, could cost you $300,000 or more.

I recommend that you make a photocopy of this list, highlight the items that you need to have completed (many computers already have some of these precautions) and give the list to your computer technician. Ask them for an estimate of the work to be completed before you leave your computer. It won't be exact, but it will give you a general idea. The price of computers has gone way down—use the additional funds to protect your PC properly.

☐ **Anti-Spyware.** Have your computer technician install and configure anti-spyware software. Installation is only one step in setting up successful software security. If it is configured (set up) incorrectly, or uses the generic factory defaults, it will not adequately protect you.

Spyware is any program that installs on your computer without your informed consent and most often adversely affects your computer's performance or forwards your personal information to advertisers, competitors or hackers.

Spyware comes in all flavors (adware, malware, etc.)—one of the more malicious forms records every keystroke you make and sends the data to those spying on you. This is one way that credit card numbers, customer records, buying habits, Social Security numbers and other pieces of identity are hijacked from your system. There are common computer symptoms that suggest your system has been infected by spyware: you receive popup ads, your computer or internet connection is running slower, your system or network is crashing more often, the default home page in your browser has recently changed without your consent, your wireless network won't connect, your computer is "acting strangely."

To minimize the impact of spyware:

• Make sure you are having a reputable software package installed. For a review of what anti-spyware software we currently suggest, visit the Reviews section of *www.thinklikeaspy.com*. We recommend that you purchase one of these packages as your primary anti-spyware software because you generally get what you pay for.

• Make sure the software has the latest security updates and is set to auto-update without user-intervention.

• Make sure the software is set to periodically run a full system scan (weekly).

• In addition, have your technician install one of the free anti-spyware programs as well (like Spy-Bot or Ad-Aware). This gives you an extra layer of protection.

☐ **Anti-Virus.** If you don't already have an anti-virus package (Norton, McAfee) installed and configured, have your computer technician do this as well.

• Make sure you are having a reputable software package installed. We review the best up-to-date packages on our website.

• Make sure it has the latest security updates and is set to auto-update without user-intervention.

• Make sure it is set to run a full system scan periodically (late at night, when you aren't using the computer).

☐ **Windows Updates.** Have your technician configure Windows for automatic security updates. Make sure that you have the latest service packs and updates for your operating system and office software. Failing to keep Windows up to date is like leaving the doors to the castle wide open.

☐ **Passwords.** Turn on Windows login passwords for each member of your family so that your private data stays private. You will still be able to share information that you want all family members to access. Have your screen saver default to the password screen after 10 minutes so that when you walk away from your computer, it is still protected (this is available from Windows XP forward).

☐ **Firewall.** A firewall is a device that regulates who (from the internet) has access into your data. It can also be used to regulate what data can leave your computer through the internet. If you connect to the internet, and especially if you have high-speed internet access (DSL, cable modem, T1), it is essential to have a firewall installed and configured. This keeps hackers from getting into your system to steal information.

Software firewalls tend to do a better job at keeping unnecessary information from leaving your computer, but they require more processing power (which means they slow your computer down) and can be a bit annoying (you are frequently asked if you want data to leave your computer over the internet).

Hardware firewalls are what most businesses use because you don't sacrifice the performance of individual computers. They can be used to block out specific websites, instant messaging and file downloads. Your computer technician should be able to make a recommendation based on your specific needs and style. We review several packages on our website.

☐ **Wireless Network.** Have your wireless network encrypted so that your data isn't floating in the airwaves for any hacker to intercept. I recommend having your technician set up WEP as well as MAC addressing. This assures that only your specific computers can get on the wireless network.

☐ **Pop-Up Blocker.** Windows now comes standard with a Pop-Up Blocker. Have your technician turn this on as it reduces the chances that you will accidentally download spyware and viruses onto your system. If you continue to get pop-ups on your computer, never click on any buttons on the screen (including the "NO" or "Decline" buttons), which will also download spyware onto your system. Instead, click on the Windows "X" at in the top right corner of your browser to close the window. Pop-ups that show up even though you have a pop-up blocker are a sure sign that your computer is infected with spyware.

☐ **Backup.** One of the most overlooked forms of security is simply making a backup copy of your data. If your computer is damaged in a fire or has a hard drive failure, the only way to get the data back is in the form of a backup copy. There are many forms of backup, but I recommend DVD burners, which will backup 8GB of data on disks that cost less than a dollar each. The initial drive should be less than $100. Make a backup of your data (e.g., your My Documents Folder) every week, or anytime you save a highly important document. Store the DVDs in your fire-safe.

☐ **Protect Your Notebook.** If you have a laptop or notebook computer, make sure you take extra precautions to protect your data. Because of their portability, notebook computers have a much higher risk of being lost or stolen. And when this happens, a thief has as long as he or she needs to break through your passwords. This could mean keeping sensitive documents off of your notebook all together, or using an encryption package like PGP that further protects your portable computer.

☐ **Good Surfing Habits.** Never click on pop-up advertisements while surfing. Stay away from danger areas such as adult entertainment. Teach your kids how to close pop-up ads (using the "X" box) as children's websites are notorious for spyware and viruses.

☐ **Secure Shopping.** When you are buying an item over the web, make sure it is with a reputable company. Also, in the bottom right corner of your browser, look for the small symbol of a closed lock, which means that the site you are buying from uses SSL encryption (which is a type of computer security that protects your data as it is transmitted). If the site is not operating on a secure server (i.e., no lock or opened lock), think twice about shopping there. Your credit card will be traveling across the internet unprotected. Either call and make the transaction over the phone or email them to see if they have a secure website where transactions can take place.

☐ Don't forget to implement the same safeguards at work and on other computers in your home.

Step 19: Protect Your PDA (Personal Digital Assistant) and Cell Phone

PDAs carry a treasure trove of information, whether they are integrated with your cell phone or independent (like a Palm Pilot). They often have passwords, Social Security numbers, bank account numbers, birthdates, addresses and phone numbers stored in them (for you and all of your contacts). Most people don't choose to turn on password protection on their phones and PDAs.

☐ Most PDAs have password protection. This tends to work well on independent devices like Palm Pilots, but not so well on phones (some of them have a tendency to lock up in mid-usage if you require a password). If you can password protect the contact management functions only (not the whole use of the phone), it seems to work better. Password protection on devices like these is quickly becoming more sophisticated, so check your cell phone or PDA manual for details.

☐ If you can't lock your phone, use the password suggestions in *Secure the Essentials* to conceal your passwords and private information.

☐ Take this information out of the PDA if you have no way to protect the data.

Step 20: Understand Phishing Scams

☐ Learn to understand and recognize phishing scams. Briefly, a phishing scam is an email disguised to look like it is from a familiar source such as your financial institution (bank or brokerage), eBay, PayPal or a host of other financial and ecommerce companies. The email asks you to login to the website by clicking on a link within the email. This link takes you to a website that looks exactly like that of the legitimate financial institution and asks you to input personal information (your identity). This information is used by the phishing thief to access your real account.

☐ Visit *www.antiphishing.org* for a better explanation of phishing, and to see real-life examples.

Step 21: Change Your Passwords and the Way You Create Them

Whether for your computer, your ATM card or a website like eBay, PayPal, your bank or brokerage, passwords are a CRUCIAL and vulnerable piece of your identity. Learn to create and protect them in the best way possible. Refer to page 82 for suggested ways to create them.

Step 22: Secure Your Vital Documents

Refer to the chart on pages 74 and 75 and take the following steps.

☐ Collect all of the documents that you need to put in a bank safe deposit box (banks charge about $50 per year for a document-sized drawer).

☐ Photocopy each of these documents and place the copy in your fire-safe or fire-rated cabinet. Keep a log of every document that lives in your bank deposit box for easy reference (especially for your spouse, who might not be as familiar with the contents).

☐ Put the documents in the bank's safety deposit box and put one key in your fire-safe and another in a completely different location (e.g., at work). Make sure that your spouse is also able to get into the safety deposit box, as they are generally sealed upon death if there are no surviving co-signers.

These documents are the most important documents in your life and should be kept indefinitely.

☐ Collect and file the remainder of the documents that belong in a fire-safe. Use one hanging file folder per year, with manila folders by subject (bank, brokerage, home, etc) to store the documents. I suggest keeping seven years of records because it is easy to remember and is an ample amount of time to store most any document. I use a slightly larger fire-rated filing cabinet so that I didn't have to purchase both a fire-safe and a locking filing cabinet.

☐ Collect and file the remainder of the documents in a locking filing cabinet. Shred any statements that have outlived their lifespan each time you file the latest documents (accumulation). Within months you will have a simplified filing cabinet.

☐ Clean up your desk, files and mail area. Use safety as a mandatory reason to clean sensitive papers off of your desk, out of drawers, etc., and centralize them in one secure location.

☐ If you own a business, make sure that your trash dumpsters are locking dumpsters. Give the trash company a key to the padlock. Locking up your trash can greatly decrease your legal liability.

Step 23: Opt-Out of Information Sharing by Your Credit Card Company

Your personal information is collected, sold and resold. It is generally used to determine credit risk or by marketing departments to sell items to you. As you learn of companies and organizations that collect your data, **OPT-OUT** of their information sharing. You opt-out by calling the number on your statement or card and asking them about their privacy policy. If they are speaking in legal gibberish, tell them that you don't want your personal information to be shared with anyone (including other subsidiaries of the same company). Ask to be removed from all junk mail and marketing lists, telemarketing lists and any other form of marketing. Ask that they no longer send "convenience checks," "courtesy checks," pre-approved credit cards or any other form of credit.

Many of the "opt-out" addresses change frequently (maybe so that people have a harder time opting out).

☐ For each credit card that you haven't cancelled, contact the issuer and tell them that you wish to opt-out of all information sharing, both within their company and with other companies.

• While you have them on the phone, ask them to stop sending you convenience checks (which are frequently stolen from mail boxes), marketing emails and telemarketing calls. Ask them who else you need to contact within the company to get off of all lists.

- Finally, ask them if you can receive your statements by email only, as these are another item routinely stolen out of unlocked mail boxes. The benefits of online statements is discussed elsewhere.

Step 24: Opt-Out of Information Sharing by Other Financial Companies

☐ Contact your insurance companies, brokerages, banks and any other financial institutions and opt-out of all information sharing. Move to online statements where possible. As statements arrive for each of these institutions, make the changes.

Step 25: Opt-Out of Telemarketing Calls

☐ Place your name on the National Do Not Call Registry. This will cut down considerably on telemarketing calls. Visit *www.donotcall.gov* and fill out the form for removing your phone numbers (home, cell, business, spouse's cell).

☐ Also place your name on the State Do Not Call Registry, if your state has one. For my home state—Colorado—you can find it at *www.coloradonocall.com* or call 1-888-249-9097. Don't forget to remove any home phone numbers as well as cell phones, business phones and your spouse's or partner's cell phone. For a list of other states, please visit our website.

Step 26: Opt-Out of Junk Mail

☐ Remove your name from the Direct Marketing Associations mailing list. This will cut down on junk mail. Visit *www.dmacon-sumers.org/cgi/offmailinglistdave* and fill out the form for removing your name. It costs $5 if you want to register online (which stops mail more quickly) or free if you mail it in. Don't forget to remove your spouse's name as well.

- While at this site, also remove your name from the Direct Marketing Associations telemarketing list. This will eliminate more telemarketing calls (even if you are on a state or national Do-Not-Call List). Visit *www.dmaconsumers.org/cgi/offtelephone* and fill out the form for removing your name. Like the mailing list, it costs $5 if you want to register online. Don't forget to remove your spouse as well.

Tip: If you are registering on both lists for you and your spouse or partner, print out the forms and send them all at once (instead of registering online). This will save you $20. It will take a little longer to get your name off of the lists, but it will save you money!

Step 27: Opt-Out of More Junk Mail

☐ There are four additional companies that sell mailing lists that you will want to contact (and more companies are being created every year to gather and market your information). You will need to contact them by mail. Make up a form letter that includes your name and address, phone number and email address. Request that you be removed from all of their mailing lists. Tell them that you want to opt out of all information sharing. The four companies you currently need to contact are:

☐ Database America, Compilation Department, 470 Chestnut Road, Woodcliff, NJ 07677

☐ Dun & Bradstreet, Customer Service, 899 Eaton Ave., Bethlehem, PA 18025

☐ Metromail Corporation, List Maintenance, 901 W. Bond, Lincoln, NE 68521

☐ R.L. Polk & Co., Name Deletion File, List Compilation Department, 26955 Northwestern Hwy, Southfield, MI 48034-4716

Step 28: Opt-Out of Search Engines

☐ Remove your phone number from Google's reverse directory. To see if your number is listed, go to *www.google.com* and type your phone number into the search window. If it comes up with your name or address, you're listed! Visit *www.google.com/help/pbremoval.html* and fill out the form to have your information removed.

☐ Remove your personal information from Zabasearch. To see if your personal information is listed, go to *www.zabasearch.com* and type your name into the search window. If it comes up with your name or address, you're listed! Email *info@zabasearch.com* with your full name and address to have your information removed. They will mail you back with a list of options that can be taken.

Many websites like Zabasearch exist that aggregate data and offer it for sale. Other examples are *anywho.com, anybirthday.com, completedetective.com* and *findsomeone.com*. The key is to remove your name from each search engine as you hear about them. To do this, simply test to see if your information is in their database (as you did above) and email them to have it removed. In many cases they will require you to mail the request (which discourages people from doing it). Make sure you mail safely. Request that they send you a confirmation of removal so that you can hold them accountable if necessary.

Step 29: Opt-Out of White Page Directories

☐ Call your local phone company and ask them to unlist your phone number when the next White Pages is published. This is where many mailing list companies collect data and sell it to other companies.

Step 30: Opt-Out of Junk Mail Catalogs

☐ To stop receiving many catalogs, email *optout@abacus-direct.com* and request that you be taken off of their lists. Include your full name and address, and the name of your spouse or partner as well.

Step 31: Opt-Out of More Junk Mail Based on Public Records

☐ Opt-out of marketing lists generated from public county property records. Visit *www.acxiom.com* and click on the Contact Us link. Once you are on the Contact Us page, use the drop-down menu that says Select a Subject and go to **U.S. Consumer Opt-Out**. This allows you to request an opt-out form that they will only send to you through the mail.

Step 32: Stop Identity Creep by Discount, Contest, Warranty and Survey

☐ Learn to say "No." Stop signing up for new credit cards, checking accounts, contests, discount cards, even if the bribe is appealing. The amount of time that you will save by keeping your identity more private and by eliminating hours opening junk mail will more than surpass the bribe you were being offered.

☐ Stop filling out Warranty Registration Cards unless it is necessary to enact the warranty (it rarely is). These cards are generally used by the marketing department of companies that want to sell your information to other businesses or sell you related items. They often request a great deal of personal information that has nothing to do with warranties.

☐ Stop completing surveys unless they are anonymous or very important to you. Check the back for a small barcode that links the survey to your identity.

Step 33: Reduce Unnecessary Internet Accounts and Website Access

☐ When you are on an internet site that will give you free content in exchange for your personal information (like newspapers, music downloads and web-support) think twice about making the trade. Is the content really worth it? If so, provide as little data as required to get the benefit, and see if it will accept generic data (John Doe, 123 Main St…). If you want to avoid further spam, give a fake email address like *abc@def.com*. If they require a confirmation email (one you have to open and respond to) you will need to give them a legitimate address. Just keep in mind the simpler you keep your response, the less identity you will have floating on the internet.

   ☐ You may want to set up a free email account (like MSN's Hotmail or YahooMail) to use when you don't want to give away your permanent email account. When setting these up, make sure that you opt-out of all shared information and, again, give as little personal data as possible.

☐ Make sure that the internet sites that you use regularly have your updated address and phone number. You don't want these companies sending statements or other information to an outdated address.

Step 34: Simplify the Documents in Your Car

☐ Clean all of the identity documents out of your glove compartment. Ideally you would lock these documents up. More practically, place your proof of insurance and car registration in an out of the way place that is easy for you to remember (like an Altoids or Band-Aid canister that fits in the compartment between your seat). Thieves that break into cars generally have to work so quickly that they won't take the extra time to search for documents that aren't in the glove compartment or behind a visor.

☐ For even greater protection, buy a "key lock" combination box like those used by real estate agents and store your sensitive documents in there. Lock the box to the car; the trunk can be a good place. If you get pulled over, explain to the police officer why you keep your information in the trunk *before* you get out of the car.

☐ Keep your repair and oil change receipts locked up in your home filing cabinet. These items are generally only needed when you are selling or have a problem with your car. They do not need to be in the car itself.

Step 35: Monitor Your Annual Social Security Statement

☐ Every year we receive an account statement from the Social Security Administration. It details your yearly earning record, expected retirement benefits and disability benefits. If your Social Security number has been stolen and someone is taking advantage of your benefits, you should be able to detect it by monitoring any changes in the statements. Make sure that your yearly Earnings Record on the statement matches your taxable income on your tax return. Verify that your benefits are increasing each year as you contribute more to retirement, not decreasing because someone is prematurely redeeming them.

☐ Make sure to have your spouse or partner monitor his or her Social Security Statement as it is completely independent of yours.

☐ Keep these statements in your dossier, or with that year's taxes.

Step 36: Photocopies, Logs & Correspondence

☐ In Chapter 5, *Simplify your Identity*, you made a copy of every piece of identity in your wallet. This copy should be stored in your dossier (which is kept in your fire-safe) and updated anytime there are significant changes. This document allows you to quickly find and contact credit card companies, motor vehicle departments, banks and other institutions that should be alerted if your wallet is lost or stolen.

☐ As you opt-out of marketing lists and information sharing, add the documents to your dossier for future reference and verification. Keep a to-do list at the start of your dossier to track any future action items and the date they need to be performed. For example, many of the opt-out programs only last for five years and need to be renewed. Write yourself a note on this page and include the date when you should renew your request.

☐ Make a log of all of the important accounts, account numbers, login names and passwords for every account you have. This should include bank accounts, brokerage accounts, insurance accounts, utilities and phone accounts and any other financial institutions that require passwords or PIN #s on their website, phone system or ATM. If your identity is stolen, you will have all of the accounts in a convenient and safe place for quick access. It also provides a centralized place for your spouse to find financial information if something should happen to you.

Step 37: Add Identity Theft Coverage to Your Homeowner's Policy

☐ Identity theft insurance is offered by many insurance companies as an endorsement on your homeowner's policy. They tend to be relatively inexpensive and cover many of the fees associated with identity theft recovery. The biggest recovery expense is usually the legal fees necessary to recover your credit and fight any criminal actions. Every company's policy is slightly different, so make sure that you understand which legal fees are covered and which are not.

The following action items are scenarios to act out in your head rather than items to check off. For a full understanding of the tools and concepts being practiced, read Chapter 8, *Observe & Evaluate* and Chapter 9, *Interrogate the Enemy*.

Step 38: Protect Your Identity at ATM machines

Scenario: You approach an ATM and pull out your wallet. You remove your debit card. Thanks to these three **triggers**, you can't help but smile to yourself as you think *SPY!*, which is a humorous but helpful warning to put your guard up. Read more about Triggers on page 95.

Your level of observation increases and you begin to evaluate the situation. You take a few seconds and look to see if anyone is watching over your shoulder to steal your PIN number. You look at the ATM machine to make sure that there aren't any devices (skimmers or hidden cameras) that aren't normally there. You look for anything out of place or any people that shouldn't be there and your instincts say that you are safe. **Stop, Look, Listen** (read more on page 98).

You are the one who approached the ATM to make a withdrawal, meaning that you have initiated the situation and are reasonably in control. You need the money and don't have time to go inside to the bank, so you make the withdrawal safely.

Step 39: Protect Your Credit Card at Restaurants & Retailers

Scenario: You are in a restaurant having dinner with friends and are about to pay the check with a credit card The waiter is going to take your credit card to another part of the restaurant to run the charges and will therefore be alone with your identity. Since you are aware that this is one of the most popular ways for thieves to steal your identity (by skimming your information on a pocket scanner), you chuckle to yourself and think *SPY!* (Note the triggers.)

You are uncertain about how to respond, because you feel like you will look foolish to your friends if you make a big deal out of letting the credit card disappear. You have several options:

☐ **Simplify Your Identity**—Pay with Cash. This old-fashioned way of paying has absolutely zero identity creep. Pay with cash when you don't want to let your card out of your sight or don't want to share information that will ultimately be stored in a database and sold to other businesses (companies buy your credit card histories so that they can market other services to you. They know that if you like to eat at certain restaurants, you will also probably buy their product).

☐ **Observe Your Card.** If the waiter stays in view, watch to make sure your card is safe. Take comfort in looking foolish from the fact that you will be safe.

☐ **Take Control—Pay at the Counter.** Take your credit card up to the cashier and pay there. That way, your card will never be out of your sight.

☐ **Do Nothing and Rely on *Plan B*.** Despite all of our training, this is probably what most of us will still do: let the card disappear with the waiter. Breaking the credit card habit seems to be particularly difficult, which means that we need another way to protect our identity when our information is out of our control. We do this by having a backup plan—a way to protect ourselves when everything else fails. Chapter 10, *Plan B*, gives us that backup plan.

Step 40: Understand What Makes Up Your Identity, see page 31

Step 41: Understand Where Identity Lives, see page 32

Step 42: Understand How Identities Are Usually Stolen, see page 35

Step 43: Understand Who Steals Identities, see page 37

Step 44: Learn about Social Engineering—the Basics of Spying, see page 106

Step 45: Understand the 6 Techniques of Interrogation, see page 109

Appendices & Endnotes

Appendix A: Helpful Resources

Here are some of the most helpful websites I found for keeping up with the latest identity theft crimes, statistics and methods of recovery:

Basic theft recovery

www.ftc.gov/idtheft

Detailed theft recovery

www.ftc.gov/bcp/conline/pubs/credit/idtheft.htm

The most current and credible statistics and prevention strategies

www.javelinstrategy.com/reports/2005IdentityFraudSurveyReport.html

State-by-state statistics

www.consumer.gov/idtheft/CY2004/statemap.pdf

Government statistics and information

www.consumer.gov/idtheft/stats.html
www.usdoj.gov/criminal/fraud/idtheft.html

Keeping track of frauds and scams

www.fraudwatchinternational.com

The latest major identity theft stories in the press

www.consumersunion.org/campaigns/financialprivacynow/newsroom.html

The best place to take legislative action

www.financialprivacynow.org

Great overall websites for consumer rights and identity theft prevention

www.privacyrights.org
www.idtheftcenter.org

Detailed information on Phishing and Pharming schemes

www.antiphishing.org

Links to the latest information, websites and resources

www.thinklikeaspy.com

Appendix B: Understanding Your Credit Report

A credit report is a record showing your credit payment history. You are assigned a credit rating or a credit score based upon your credit payment history. These documents (one from each of the three credit bureaus) are probably the most important means of detecting identity theft.

When evaluating a credit report you should look for consistency. I like the 3-in-1 reports that give you all of the information from each agency in one easy report. The Equifax Credit Watch Gold with 3-in-1 Monitoring is a good example available at *www.equifax.com*.

Once you have obtained access to the report, look for accounts you don't have, inquiries you didn't make, credit cards you didn't open, residences you never lived at, court actions in other states, or unexpected changes to your credit rating.

Sections of a credit report:

Personal Information—A personal profile

- Names
- Residences (Current and Previous)
- Social Security Number
- Date of Birth
- Driver's License Number
- Telephone Numbers
- Spouse's Name
- Employer's Name and Address

Any discrepancies with the information in your credit report could be a sign of fraud. You should file a dispute with the credit bureau for all your personal information discrepancies.

Credit Summary—History of all opened and closed accounts under your name:

- Source (i.e., Bank Name/Address)
- Date Opened/Reported Since
- Type/Terms/Monthly Payment
- Responsibility
- Credit Limit/Original Amount/High Balance
- Recent Balance/Recent Payment
- Status Details

Lenders are not required to send your information to all three bureaus, so loans are sometimes only reported to one bureau, which can create discrepancies between different credit reports. In addition, some reports provide a history of balances for each of the lenders while others do not. It is important to get a 3-in-1 report to see if any fraudulent accounts have been opened under your name. Any accounts you didn't open or any loans that are not yours should be disputed.

Public Records—Court actions coming from federal, state, and county court records:

- Bankruptcy
- Tax Liens
- Monetary Judgments
- Overdue Child Support Payments

If you find any discrepancies such as court actions from states you have not lived in, file a dispute with the bureau.

Credit Inquiries—There are two types of inquiries, Hard and Soft:

- Hard Inquiries—You initiate the inquiry by filling out a credit application. These inquiries influence your credit rating and should be kept to a minimum.

- Soft Inquiries—These inquiries include pre-approved credit cards or pre-employment screenings and can only be seen by you. They do not affect your credit rating.

If you did not apply for a loan or credit card that appears in this section, file a dispute with the bureau.

Credit Rating/Credit Score—Provides an indication to lenders of your credit risk:

- All three credit bureaus use their own rating system (Equifax— BEACON, Experian—Fair Isaac Risk Model, TransUnion— EMPIRICA)

- The higher your score, the better your credit rating

Your credit rating is affected positively and negatively by many factors, for example:

Positive Factors	Negative Factors
Associations with three or more creditors	Too many inquiries in the last two years
No disparaging information	Too many installment loans (car loans or college loans)
Accounts opened for five or more years	Too many installment loans (car loans or college loans)
Credit balances that are not close to your card limit	Credit balances that are too close to your card limit
Few or zero delinquencies of 30 or more days	Delinquencies of 30 or more days

Note: If your credit score has unexpectedly changed, this could be a sign of fraud.

Endnotes

1. *2005 Identity Fraud Survey Report*, Javelin Strategy & Research, p. 3.

2. According to the *2005 Identity Fraud Survey Report* conducted by Javelin Strategy & Research, 9.3 million American adults became victims of identity theft in 2004. Based on the percent of the U.S. adult population, 4.25% of adults had their identity stolen in one year. In 2003, the percentage was 4.7%. Together, these figures add up to 8.95%. I derive my 1 in 10 approximation by adding in 1% for identity theft cases that went unreported. This number is substantially below actual estimates, but I have defaulted on the conservative side.

3. *2005 Identity Fraud Survey Report*, Javelin Strategy & Research, p. 4.

4. *2005 Identity Fraud Survey Report*, Javelin Strategy & Research, p. 6.

5. *2005 Identity Fraud Survey Report*, Javelin Strategy & Research, p. 3.

6. See *California v. Greenwood*, US Citation 486 U.S. 35 (1988) Docket 86-684, Conclusion: Voting 6 to 2, the Court held that garbage placed at the curbside is unprotected by the Fourth Amendment. The Court argued that there was no reasonable expectation of privacy for trash on public streets "readily accessible to animals, children, scavengers, snoops, and other members of the public." The Court also noted that the police cannot be expected to ignore criminal activity that can be observed by "any member of the public."

7. *2005 Identity Fraud Survey Report*, Javelin Strategy & Research, p. 2. Please note that the 50% figure refers only to the percentage of cases where the victims knew how their identity was stolen. Many people never know how their identity was stolen and those people are not represented in this number.

8. *2005 Identity Fraud Survey Report*, Javelin Strategy & Research, p. 10.

9. Better Business Bureau/Javelin Strategy & Research Press Release,

San Francisco, January 26, 2005, p. 3.

10. *2005 Identity Fraud Survey Report,* Javelin Strategy & Research, p. 3.

11. Better Business Bureau/Javelin Strategy & Research Press Release, San Francisco, January 26, 2005, p. 3.

12. *2005 Identity Fraud Survey Report,* Javelin Strategy & Research, p. 9.

13. Better Business Bureau/Javelin Strategy & Research Press Release, San Francisco, January 26, 2005, p. 3.

14. *2005 Identity Fraud Survey Report,* Javelin Strategy & Research, p. 4.

15. *2005 Identity Fraud Survey Report,* Javelin Strategy & Research, p. 7.

Index

We must make privacy a HABIT,
not a one-time checklist.

We must understand the ENEMY
to protect ourselves.

We must learn to THINK critically
about our privacy.

We must take ACTION in
gradual, organized steps.

Quick Order Form

Website Orders: www.thinklikeaspy.com

Email Orders: orders@thinklikeaspy.com

Fax Orders: 1-866-422-4922 (toll free)

Telephone Orders: 1-866-SPYTHINK (779-8446)

Postal Orders: Book Orders, 381 S. Broadway, Denver, CO 80209-1522, USA

Please contact me about:

☐ Speaking engagements   ☐ Consulting

☐ Seminars/Workshops   ☐ Other Books

Name: _____

Address: _____

_____

City: _____

State: _____Zip: _____

Telephone: _____

Email: _____

Number of Books _____@ $14.95 ea. = $ _____

Tax: Please add 7.6% for products shipped to
Colorado addresses. $ _____

Shipping Add $3.95 first book/$2.00 each additional. $ _____

International Shipping: US$9.00 for first book and
US$5.00 for each additional product (estimate). $ _____

TOTAL $ _____

Payment: ☐ Check   ☐ Visa/MasterCard/Amex/Discover/Optima

Card Number: _____

Exp. Date:_____Signature _____

About the Author

 During 2003, John Sileo's identity was stolen and used to commit a series of crimes, including $300,000 worth of embezzlement. While the thief operated behind the safety of John's identity, John was held legally and financially responsible for the felonies committed. Forced to defend his innocence, John spent two stressful years and $9,000 on a criminal lawyer to keep from going to jail.

During that time, John became an expert in identity theft prevention and mitigation strategies. The methods of survival he developed during this experience are the basis of this book, and are responsible for the successful capture and conviction of his imposter.

John is often asked to speak to associations, corporations and consumers about identity theft prevention and broader issues of privacy. His company provides consulting services to businesses that wish to proactively protect private information. By applying **Think Like a Spy**™ methodologies developed for this book, John trains corporations on how to quickly detect and deter data theft and financial fraud on all rungs of the corporate ladder (from the mailroom to the boardroom).

John graduated with honors from Harvard University and served as a Rotary Ambassadorial Scholar to New Zealand. He is the founder of four successful businesses and the acting president of two others. He lives with his wife and two daughters in Colorado.

You can book a speech or reach John at *john@thinklikeaspy.com,* by visiting *www.thinklikeaspy.com* or by calling toll-free 1-866-SPY-THINK (866-779-8446).

Please Note: All requests for bulk purchases of Stolen Lives should be made by calling 1-866-SPY-THINK (866-779-8446). Bulk pricing is available for Banks, Credit Card Companies, Insurance Companies, Corporations and Associations committed to protecting their customers, members, employees and information assets.